Birds of Indiana

Field Guide

D0932179

by Stan Tekiela

ADVENTURE PUBLICATIONS
CAMBRIDGE, MINNESOTA

To my wife Katherine and daughter Abigail with all my love

ACKNOWLEDGMENTS:

Special thanks to Indiana birders John Castrale and Charles Keller for reviewing the range maps.

Edited by Sandy Livoti

Book design and illustrations by Jonathan Norberg

Range maps produced by Anthony Hertzel

Photo credits by photographer and page number:

Cover photo: Northern Flicker by Warren Nelson
Brian Collins: 116, 156, 212, 220, 230 **Cornell Laboratory of Ornithology**: 58, 60 (female), 192 (both) **Dudley Edmondson**: 14, 16 (soaring), 42 (soaring), 44, 46 (all), 64, 68, 74, 80, 88 (both), 112 (in flight), 122 (both), 124 (male), 128, 136 (soaring), 150 (both), 154, 172 (male), 182, 190 (male), 194 (perching, soaring), 196, 200, 236 (breeding), 238 (breeding), 248 (male, winter male), 250, 254 (male), 260 **Carrol Henderson**: 82, 114 (female), 244, 252 (female) **Kevin T. Karlson**: 34, 114 (female), 244, 252 (female) **Bill Marchel**: 22 (male), 30, 60 (male), 72, 90 (white-striped), 94, 118, 132, 136 (perching), 142, 146, 158 (female), 172 (female), 206, 208 (both), 214, 216, 222, 228, 234, 240 **Maslowski Wildlife Productions**: 20, 62, 66 (soaring), 76, 108 (male, female), 162, 164, 170, 184, 232, 246, 256, 258 **Arthur Morris**: 114 (male) **Steve Mortensen**: 22 (female), 26 (male), 28 (both), 38 (both), 40, 42 (perching), 48, 52, 54 (both), 84, 86 (both), 138, 144, 148, 178, 180, 210, 248 (female), 264 (both) **Warren Nelson**: 26 (female), 124 (female), 254 (female) **John Pennoyer**: 70, 218, 226 **Brian E. Small**: 106 (winter), 134, 224, 236 (winter, juvenile), 238 (winter), 252 (male), 262 **Stan Tekiela**: 2, 4, 6 (both), 8, 10, 12, 18 (all), 24, 32 (both), 36, 50, 56 (both), 66 (perching), 78, 90 (tan-striped), 92 (both), 96, 98 (adult, 1 year old), 100, 102, 104, 106 (breeding), 108 (juvenile), 110, 112 (perching), 120, 126, 130, 140, 152, 158 (male), 160, 166 (both), 168, 174, 176, 186, 188 (gray morph), 190 (female), 194 (juvenile), 202, 204, 242 (both), 266 **Brian Wheeler**: 16 (perching), 198 (all) **Jim Zipp**: 98 (Bohemian), 188 (red morph)

To the best of the publisher's knowledge, all photos but one were of live birds. Due to the elusive nature of the female Indigo Bunting, the only available photo that met identification criteria was of a mounted bird.

10 9 8

Copyright 2000 by Stan Tekiela
Published by Adventure Publications, Inc.
820 Cleveland St. S
Cambridge, MN 55008
1-800-678-7006
www.adventurepublications.net
Printed in China

ISBN: 978-1-885061-90-4

TABLE OF CONTENTS

Introduction

Sample Page

The Birds

Helpful Resources

Check List/Index

About the Author

WHY WATCH BIRDS IN INDIANA?

Millions of people have discovered bird feeding. It's a simple and enjoyable way to bring the beauty of birds closer to your home. Watching birds at your feeder often leads to a lifetime pursuit of bird identification. The *Birds of Indiana Field Guide* is for those who want to identify common birds of Indiana.

There are more than 800 species of birds found in North America. In Indiana alone there have been over 375 different kinds of birds recorded over the years. These bird sightings were diligently recorded by hundreds of bird watchers and became part of the official state record. From these valuable records, I have chosen 112 of the most common birds of Indiana to include in this field guide.

Bird watching, often called birding, is the largest spectator sport in America. Its outstanding popularity in Indiana is due, in part, to an unusually rich and abundant birdlife. Why are there so many birds? One reason is open space. Indiana is more than 36,000 square miles (94,000 sq. km), making it the thirty-eighth largest state. Despite its size, only about 6 million people call Indiana home. That is only 152 people per square mile (59 per sq. km). Most of these people are located in Indiana's five major cities.

Open space is not the only reason there is such an abundance of birds. It's also the diversity of habitat. The state can be broken into three distinct regions (north, central and south), each of which supports a different group of birds. Water also plays a big part of Indiana bird populations. The state shares a portion of Lake Michigan on its northwestern corner. The southern border is formed by the Ohio River, and the southwest border by the Wabash River.

The glaciated northern zone of Indiana has gentle rolling hills and also contains most of the natural lakes, sand dunes and peat bogs, and is home to birds such as the Rose-breasted Grosbeak.

It is also a good place to see some of the "winter finches" such as the Purple Finch.

The central portion of the state, which was originally a prairie habitat and is now agricultural, has many open country birds such as the Horned Lark and Eastern Meadowlark. The rivers of central Indiana are lined with deep rich forests that harbor many birds, including many kinds of waterfowl.

Southern Indiana is known for its extensive tracts of forest and winding rivers. The forested valleys and ridges are home for many birds such as the Great Crested Flycatcher.

Besides the varying habitat, Indiana has varying weather. Since the state extends over 275 miles (443 km) from north to south, the weather ranges greatly. From the cold winters on the northern Michigan border to the steamy summers of southern Indiana, there are birds to watch in every season. Whether witnessing a migration of hawks in the fall or welcoming back the hummingbirds in the spring, there is variety and excitement in birding as each season turns to the next.

OBSERVE WITH A STRATEGY; TIPS FOR IDENTIFYING BIRDS

Identifying birds isn't as difficult as you might think. If you follow just a few basic strategies, you can increase your chances of successfully identifying most birds you see! One of the first and easiest things to do when you see a new bird is to note its color. (Also, since this book is organized by color, you will go right to that color section to find it.)

Next, note the size of the bird. A strategy to quickly estimate size is to select a small-, medium- and large-sized bird to use for reference. For example, most people are familiar with robins. A robin, measured from the tip of its bill to the tip of its tail, is ten inches long. Using the robin as an example of a medium-sized bird, select two other birds, one smaller and one larger. Many people use a House Sparrow, at about 6 inches, and an American Crow, about 18 inches. When you see a bird that you don't know, you can quickly ask yourself, "Is it smaller than a robin, but larger than a sparrow?" When you look in your field guide to help identify your bird, you'll know it's roughly between six and ten inches long. This will help narrow your choices.

Next, note the size, shape and color of the bill. Is it long, thin, pointed, short, thick, blunt, curved or straight? Seed-eating birds, such as the Northern Cardinal, have bills that are thick and strong enough to crack even the toughest seeds. Birds that sip nectar, like Ruby-throated Hummingbirds, need long thin bills to reach deep into flowers. Hawks and owls tear their prey with very sharp, curved bills. Sometimes, just noting the bill shape can help you decide if the bird is a woodpecker, finch, grosbeak or blackbird.

Next, take a look around and note the habitat in which you see the bird. Is it wading in a marsh? Walking along a riverbank? Soaring in the sky? Is it perched high in the trees or hopping along the forest floor? Because of their preferences in diet and habitat, you'll usually see robins hopping on the ground, but not often eating the seeds at your feeder. Or you'll see a Rose-breasted Grosbeak sitting on the branches of a tree, but not climbing down the tree trunk the way a nuthatch does.

Noticing what a bird is eating will give you another clue to help you identify that bird. Feeding is a big part of any bird's life. Fully one-third of all bird activities revolves around searching for and catching food, or actually eating. While birds don't always follow all the rules of what we think they eat, you can make some general assumptions. Northern Flickers, for instance, feed upon ants and other insects, so you wouldn't expect to see them visiting a backyard bird feeder. Some birds, such as Barn and Tree Swallows, feed on flying insects, and spend hours swooping and diving to catch a meal.

Sometimes you can identify a bird by the way it is perched. Body posture can help you to differentiate between an American Crow and a Red-tailed Hawk. American Crows lean forward over their feet when perched on a branch, while hawks perch in an upright or vertical position. Look for this the next time you see a large unidentified bird in a tree.

Birds in flight are often difficult to identify, but noting the size and shape of the wing will help. A bird's wing size is in direct proportion to its body size, weight and type of flying. The shape of the wing determines if the bird flies fast and with precision, or slowly and less precisely. Birds such as House Finches, which flit around a thick tangle of branches, have short round wings. Birds that soar on warm updrafts of air, such as Turkey Vultures, have wings that are long and broad. Barn Swallows have short pointed wings that slice through the air, propelling their swift and accurate flight.

Some birds have unique flight patterns that aid in identification. American Goldfinches fly in a distinctive up-and-down pattern that makes it look as if they are riding a roller coaster.

While it's not easy to make these observations in the short time you often have to watch a "mystery bird," practicing these methods of identification will greatly expand your birding skills. Also, seek the guidance of a more experienced birder who will help you improve your skills and answer your questions on the spot.

BIRD BASICS

It's easier to identify birds and communicate about them if you know the names of the different parts of a bird. For instance, it's much easier to use the word "crest" to describe the erect feathers on the head of a Northern Cardinal than trying to describe it.

The following illustration points out the basic parts of a bird. Because it's a composite of many birds, it should not be confused with any actual bird.

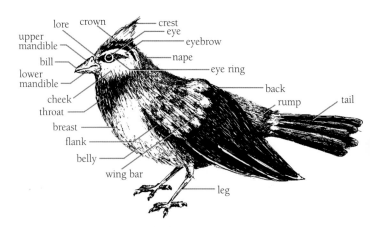

BIRD COLOR VARIABLES

No other animal has a color pallet like a bird's. Vivid blues, lemon yellows, intense reds and iridescent greens are commonplace within the bird world. In general, male birds are more colorful than their female counterparts. This is probably to help the male attract a mate, essentially saying, "Hey, look at me!" It also calls attention to the male's overall health. The better the condition of his feathers, the better his food source and territory, and therefore, the better his potential for a mate.

Females that don't look like their male counterparts (such species are called sexually dimorphic, meaning "two forms") are often a nondescript brown color, as seen with Rose-breasted Grosbeaks. These muted tones help to hide the females during weeks of motionless incubation, and draw less attention to her when she is out feeding or taking a break from the rigors of raising her young.

In some species, such as the Bald Eagle, Blue Jay and Downy Woodpecker, the male birds look nearly identical to the females. In the case of the woodpeckers, the sexes are only differentiated by a single red or sometimes yellow mark. Depending on the species, the mark may be on top of the head, face, nape of the neck or just behind the bill.

During the first year, juvenile birds often look like the mothers. Since brightly colored feathers are used mainly for attracting a mate, young non-breeding males don't have a need for colorful plumage. This also helps protect them while they are young. It is not until the first spring molt, or even several years later, depending on the species, that the young males obtain their breeding colors.

MOLTING

All birds molt. Molting is the process of dropping old worn feathers and replacing them with new ones. Typically, a bird will molt twice a year, with the first molt, or spring molt, usually occurring in late winter. During this molt the birds produce their breeding plumage (brighter colors for attracting mates), which will carry them through the summer. The second, or summer molt, serves two important functions. First, it adds additional feathers for warmth in the coming winter. Second, the winter plumage tends to be drab in color, such as that of the male American Goldfinch, which changes from canary yellow to olive brown. Luckily for us, some birds, such as the male Northern Cardinal, retain their bright summer color all year long.

BIRD NESTS

Bird nests are truly an amazing feat of engineering. Just imagine building your home strong enough to weather a storm, large enough to hold your entire family, warm enough to shelter them from the cold and waterproof enough to keep out rain. Now, build it without any blueprints or directions, and without the use of your hands or feet! Birds do!

Before building a nest, an appropriate site must be selected. With some birds, such as the House Wren, the male picks out several potential sites and assembles several small twigs in each. This discourages other birds from using nearby nest cavities. These "extra" nests are sometimes called dummy nests. The female is then taken around and shown all the choices. She chooses her favorite and finishes constructing the nest. With some other species of birds, for example, Baltimore Orioles, it's the female who chooses the site and builds the nest with the male only offering an occasional suggestion. Each bird species has its own nest-building routine, which is strictly followed.

Nesting material usually consists of natural elements found in the immediate area. Most nests consist of plant fibers (such as bark peeled from grapevines), sticks, mud, dried grass, feathers, fur, or soft fuzzy tufts from thistle. Some birds, including Ruby-throated Hummingbirds, use spider webs to glue nest materials together. Nesting material is limited to what a bird can hold or carry. Because of this, a bird must make many trips afield to gather enough materials to complete its nest. Most nests take at least four days or more, and hundreds, if not thousands, of trips to build.

As you'll see in the following illustrations, birds build a wide variety of nest types.

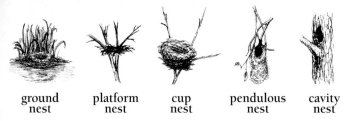

| ground nest | platform nest | cup nest | pendulous nest | cavity nest |

The simple **ground nest** is scraped out of the earth. These shallow depressions usually contain no nesting material, and are made by birds such as the Killdeer and Horned Lark.

Another type of nest, the **platform nest**, represents a more complex type of nest building. Constructed of small twigs and branches, the platform nest is a simple arrangement of sticks which forms a platform and features a small depression to nestle the eggs.

Some platform nests, such as those of the Common Loon, are constructed on the ground, and are made of mud and grass. Platform nests can also be on cliffs, bridges, balconies or even in flowerpots. This kind of nest gives space to adventurous youngsters, and functions as a landing platform for the parents. Many waterfowl construct platform nests on the ground, usually near water or actually in the water. These floating platform nests vary with the water level, thus preventing nests with eggs from being flooded. Platform nests, constructed by such birds as Mourning Doves and herons, are not anchored to the tree, and may tumble from the branches during high winds and storms.

The **cup nest** is a modified platform nest, used by three-quarters of all songbirds. Constructed from the outside in, a supporting platform is constructed first. This platform is attached firmly to a tree, shrub, rock ledge or the ground. Next, the sides are constructed of grasses, small twigs, bark or leaves, which are woven together and often glued with mud for additional strength. The inner cup, lined with feathers, animal fur, soft plant material or animal hair, is constructed last. The mother bird uses her chest to cast the final contours of the inner nest.

The **pendulous nest** is an unusual nest, looking more like a sock hanging from a branch than a nest. Inaccessible to most predators, these nests are attached to the ends of the smallest branches of a tree, and often wave wildly in the breeze. Woven very tightly of plant fibers, they are strong and water tight, taking up to a week to build. More commonly used by tropical birds, this complicated nest type has also been mastered by orioles and kinglets. A small opening on the top or side allows the parents access to the grass-lined interior. (It must be one heck of a ride to be inside one of these nests during a windy spring thunderstorm!)

Another nest type, the **cavity nest**, is used by many birds, including woodpeckers and Eastern Bluebirds. The cavity nest is usually excavated in a tree branch or trunk, and offers shelter from the storms, sun, predators and the cold of Indiana's climate. A relatively small entrance hole in a tree leads to an inner chamber up to ten inches below. In some cases, a four-foot tunnel connects the entrance in a riverbank to the nest chamber. These nests are often sparsely lined because they are well insulated. Usually constructed by woodpeckers and kingfishers, the cavity nest is used only once by its builder, but can be used for many years by birds such as the Common Goldeneye, mergansers and bluebirds, which do not have the capability of excavating one for themselves.

One of the most clever of all nest types is known as the **no nest** or daycare nest. Parasitic birds, like the Brown-headed Cowbird, build no nests at all! The egg-laden female expertly searches out other birds' nests and sneaks in to lay one of her own eggs while the host mother is not looking, thereby leaving the host mother to raise an adopted youngster. The mother cowbird wastes no energy building a nest only to have it raided by a predator. By using several nests of other birds, she spreads out her progeny in hope that at least one of her offspring will live to maturity.

Some birds, including some swallows, take nest building one step further. They use a collection of small balls of mud to construct an adobe-style home. Constructed under the eaves of houses, under bridges or inside chimneys, some of these nests look like simple cup nests. Others are completely enclosed, with small tunnel-like openings that lead into a safe nesting chamber for the baby birds.

WHO BUILDS THE NEST?

In general, the female bird builds the nest. She gathers nesting materials and constructs a nest, with an occasional visit from her mate to check on the progress. In some species, both parents contribute equally to the construction of a nest. A male bird might forage for precisely the right sticks, grass or mud, but it's often the female that forms or puts together the nest. She uses her body to form the egg chamber. Rarely does the male build a nest by himself.

FLEDGING

Fledging is the interval between hatching and flight or leaving the nest. Some birds leave the nest within hours of hatching, but it might be weeks before they are able to fly. This is common with waterfowl. Until they start to fly, they are called fledglings. Birds that are still in the nest are called nestlings.

WHY BIRDS MIGRATE

Why do birds migrate? The short answer is simple—food. Birds migrate to areas of high food concentrations. It is easier to breed where food is than where it is not. A typical migrating bird, the Rose-breasted Grosbeak, for instance, migrates from the tropics of Central and South America to nest in the forests of North America, taking advantage of billions of newly hatched insects to feed its young. This trip is called **complete migration**.

Some birds of prey return from their complete migration to northern regions that are overflowing with small rodents, such as mice and voles, that have continued to breed in winter.

Complete migrators have a set time and pattern of migration. Each year at nearly the same time, they take off and head for a specific wintering ground. Complete migrators may travel incredible distances, sometimes as much as 15,000 miles or more in one year. But complete migration doesn't necessarily imply flying from the cold and frozen northland to some tropical destination. Dark-eyed Junco, for example, is a complete migrator that flies from the far reaches of Canada to spend the winter right here in Indiana.

There are many interesting aspects to complete migrators. In the spring, males usually migrate several weeks before the females, arriving early to scope out possible nesting sites and food sources, and to begin to defend territories. The females arrive several weeks later. In the autumn, in many species, the females and their young leave early, often up to four weeks before the adult males.

Not all migrators are the same. There are **partial migrators**, such as American Goldfinches, that usually wait until food supplies dwindle before they fly south. Unlike complete migrators, the partial migrators move only far enough south, or sometimes east and west, to find abundant food. Some years it might be only a few hundred miles, while other years it might be nearly a thousand. This kind of migration, dependent upon the weather and available food, is sometimes called **seasonal movement**.

Unlike the predictable ebbing and flowing behavior of the complete migrators or partial migrators, **irruptive migrators** can move every third to fifth year, or in some cases, in consecutive years. These migrations are triggered when times are really tough and food is scarce. Red-breasted Nuthatches are a good example of irruptive migrators, because they leave their normal northern range in search of food or in response to overpopulation.

How Do Birds Migrate?

One of the many secrets of migration is fat. While we humans are fighting the battle of the bulge, birds intentionally gorge themselves to put on as much fat as possible while still being able to fly. Fat provides the greatest amount of energy per unit of weight, and in the same way that your car needs gas, birds are propelled by fat or stalled without it.

During long migratory flights, fat deposits are used up quickly, and birds need to stop to "refuel." This is when backyard bird feeding stations and undeveloped, natural spaces around our towns and cities are especially important. Some birds require up to two to three days of constant feeding to build up their fat reserves before continuing their seasonal trip.

Some birds, such as most eagles, hawks, ospreys, falcons and vultures, migrate during the day. Larger birds can hold more body fat, go longer without eating and take longer to migrate. These birds glide along on rising columns of warm air, called thermals, which hold them aloft while they slowly make their way south. They generally rest at night and hunt early in the morning before the sun has a chance to warm up the land and create good soaring conditions. Birds migrating during the day use a combination of landforms, rivers, and the rising and set-ting sun to guide them in the right direction.

Most birds migrate during the night. Studies show that birds which migrate at night use the stars to navigate. Others use the setting sun, while still others, such as doves, use the earth's mag-netic fields to guide them south. While flying at night might seem like a crazy idea, nocturnal migration is safer for several reasons. First, there are fewer nighttime predators for migrating birds. Second, traveling at night allows time during the day to find food in unfamiliar surroundings. Finally, nighttime wind patterns tend to be flat, or laminar. These winds don't have the turbulence associated with daytime winds, and can actually help carry smaller birds by pushing them along.

HOW TO USE THIS GUIDE

To help you quickly and easily identify birds, this book is organized by color. Simply note the color of the bird and turn to that section. Refer to the first page for the color key. The male Rose-breasted Grosbeak, for example, is black-and-white with a red patch on its chest. Because the bird is mostly black and white, it will be found in the black and white section. Each color section is also arranged by size, generally with the smaller birds first. Sections may also incorporate the average size in a range, which in some cases reflects size differences between male and female birds. Flip through the pages in that color section to find the bird. If you already know the name of the bird, check the index for the page number. In some species, the male and female are remarkably different in color. In these cases, the opposite sex is shown in a smaller inset photograph with a page reference. These birds, therefore, will be found in two different color sections.

In the description section you will find a variety of information about the bird. On the following page is a sample of the information included in the book.

RANGE MAPS

Range maps are included for each bird. The colored areas indicate where in Indiana a particular bird is most likely to be found. The colors represent the presence of a species during a specific season, not the density or amount of birds in the area. Green is used for summer, blue for winter, red for year-round and yellow for areas where the bird is seen during migration. While every effort has been made to accurately depict the ranges, they are only general guidelines. Ranges actually change on an ongoing basis due to a variety of factors. Changes in the weather, species abundance, landscape and vital resources such as the availability of food and water can affect local populations, migration and movements, causing birds to be found in areas that are atypical for the species.

The colored areas simply mean bird sightings for that species have been frequent in those areas and less frequent in the others. Please use the maps as intended–as general guides only.

COMMON NAME
Scientific name

Size: measured from head to tail

Male: a brief description of the male bird

Female: a brief description of the female bird, which is sometimes not the same as the male

Juvenile: a brief description of the juvenile bird, which often looks like the female

Nest: the kind of nest this bird builds to raise its young, who builds the nest, and how many broods per year

Eggs: how many eggs you might expect to see in a nest, and the color of the eggs

Incubation: the average time the parents spend incubating the eggs, and who does the incubation

Fledging: the average time the young spend in the nest after hatching but before they leave the nest, and which parent(s) does most of the "child-care" and feeding

Migration: type of migration: complete (consistent, seasonal), or partial (seasonal, destination varies), or irruptive (unpredictable, depending on the food supply), or non-migrator (the general location where the bird spends the winter)

Food: what the bird eats most of the time (e.g., seeds, nectar, insects, fruit, small animals), and if it typically comes to a bird feeding station

Compare: notes about other birds that look similar, and the pages on which they can be found

Stan's Notes: Interesting gee-whiz natural history information. This could be something to look or listen for, or something to help positively identify the bird. Also includes remarkable features.

female
pg. 97

male

EASTERN TOWHEE
Pipilo erythrophthalmus

YEAR-ROUND
SUMMER

Size: 7-8" (18-20 cm)

Male: A mostly black bird with dirty red brown sides and white belly. Long black tail with white tip. Short, stout, pointed bill with rich red eye. White wing patches flash in flight.

Female: similar to male, but is brown, not black

Juvenile: light brown, heavily streaked head, chest and belly, long dark tail with white tip

Nest: cup; female builds; 2 broods per year

Eggs: 3-4; creamy white with brown markings

Incubation: 12-13 days; female incubates

Fledging: 10-12 days; female and male feed young

Migration: complete, to southern states and South America

Food: insects, seeds, fruit, comes to ground feeder

Compare: Slightly smaller than the American Robin (pg. 191). The Gray Catbird (pg. 187) lacks a black "hood" and rusty sides. Common Grackle (pg. 11) lacks white belly and has long thin bill. Male Rose-breasted Grosbeak (pg. 25) has a rosy patch in center of chest.

Stan's Notes: Common name comes from its distinctive "tow-hee" call given by both sexes. Mostly known for its characteristic call that sounds like, "Drink-your-tea!" White-eyed form in southern states. Seen hopping backward with both feet to rake up leaf litter, called bilateral scratching, in search of insects and seeds. Female broods, but male does most of the feeding of young.

3

female
pg. 101

male

BROWN-HEADED COWBIRD
Molothrus ater

YEAR-ROUND

Size: 7½" (19 cm)

Male: A glossy black bird, reminiscent of a Red-winged Blackbird. Chocolate brown head with a pointed, sharp gray bill.

Female: dull brown bird with bill similar to male

Juvenile: similar to female, only duller gray with streaked chest

Nest: no nest; lays eggs in nests of other birds

Eggs: 5-7; white with brown markings

Incubation: 10-13 days; host bird incubates eggs

Fledging: 10-11 days; host birds feed young

Migration: complete, to southern states

Food: insects, seeds, will come to seed feeders

Compare: In the blackbird family. The slightly larger male Red-winged Blackbird (pg. 9) has red and yellow markings on wings. Common Grackle (pg. 11) has a long tail, but lacks brown head. European Starling (pg. 7) has yellow bill and shorter tail.

Stan's Notes: Of about 750 species of parasitic birds worldwide, this is the only parasitic bird in Indiana, laying all eggs in host birds' nests, leaving others to raise its young. Cowbirds are known to have laid eggs in nests of over 200 species of birds. Some birds reject cowbird eggs, but most raise them, even to the exclusion of their own young. Look for warblers and other birds feeding young birds twice their own size. At one time they followed bison to feed on the insects attracted to the animals.

winter

breeding

EUROPEAN STARLING
Sturnus vulgaris

YEAR-ROUND

Size: 7½" (19 cm)

Male: An iridescent purple black bird covered with white speckles during fall and winter. Shiny purple black in spring and summer. Long, pointed gray bill in autumn and yellow in spring. Short tail.

Female: same as male

Juvenile: similar to adult, only gray brown with streaked chest

Nest: cavity; male and female line cavity; 2 broods per year

Eggs: 4-6; bluish with brown markings

Incubation: 12-14 days; female and male incubate

Fledging: 18-20 days; female and male feed young

Migration: non-migrator to partial migrator, some will move to southern states

Food: insects, seeds, fruit, will come to seed and suet feeders

Compare: Looks similar to Common Grackle (pg. 11), but lacks its long tail.

Stan's Notes: Great songsters, they are also able to mimic sounds. Often displaces woodpeckers, chickadees and other cavity-nesting birds. Can be very aggressive and destroy eggs or young of other birds. The bill changes color with the seasons: yellow in spring and gray in autumn. Jaws are designed to be most powerful when opening, as they pry open crevices to locate hidden insects. Gathers in the hundreds in autumn. Not a native bird, they were introduced to New York City in 1890-91 from Europe.

male

RED-WINGED BLACKBIRD
Agelaius phoeniceus

Size: 8½" (22 cm)

Male: Jet black bird with red and yellow shoulder patch on upper wing. Pointed black bill.

Female: heavily streaked brown bird with white eyebrow, brown bill

Juvenile: same as female

Nest: cup; female builds; 2-3 broods per year

Eggs: 3-4; bluish green with brown markings

Incubation: 10-12 days; female incubates

Fledging: 11-14 days; female and male feed young

Migration: complete, to southern states, Mexico and Central America

Food: insects, seeds, will come to seed feeders

Compare: Slightly larger than the male Brown-headed Cowbird (pg. 5), but is less iridescent and lacks Cowbird's brown head. Differs from all blackbirds due to the red and yellow patches on its wings, called epaulets.

Stan's Notes: It is a sure sign of spring when the Red-winged Blackbirds return to the marsh. Flocks of up to 100,000 birds have been reported. Males return before females and defend territories. Will repeat call from top of cattail while showing off red and yellow wing bars, called epaulets. Females choose mate. Nests are usually over shallow water in thick stand of cattails. One of the most wide-spread and numerous birds in Indiana. Feeds mostly on seeds in spring and fall, switching to insects during summer.

YEAR-ROUND

COMMON GRACKLE
Quiscalus quiscula

Size:	11-13" (28-33 cm)
Male:	Large black bird with iridescent blue black head, purple brown body, long black tail, long thin bill and bright golden eyes.
Female:	similar to male, only duller and smaller
Juvenile:	similar to female
Nest:	cup; female builds; 2 broods per year
Eggs:	4-5; greenish white with brown markings
Incubation:	13-14 days; female incubates
Fledging:	16-20 days; female and male feed young
Migration:	complete, to southern states
Food:	fruit, seeds, insects, comes to seed feeders
Compare:	European Starling (pg. 7) is much smaller and has a speckled appearance and yellow bill. Male Red-winged Blackbird (pg. 9) has red and yellow wing markings.

Stan's Notes: Usually nests in small colonies of up to 75 pairs. Travels with other blackbirds in large flocks. Known to feed in farmers' fields. Their name comes from the Latin word *graculus*, meaning "to cough," for their loud raspy call. Male holds tail in a vertical keel-like position during flight. Flight pattern is almost always level, as opposed to undulated up-and-down movements. Unlike most birds, has larger muscles to open mouth rather than to close it, as it pries open crevices to locate hidden insects.

YEAR-ROUND

AMERICAN COOT
Fulica americana

Size: 13-16" (33-40 cm)

Male: Slate gray-to-black all over, white bill with dark band near tip. Green legs and feet. Small white patch near the base of tail. Prominent red eye and a small red patch above bill between eyes.

Female: same as male

Juvenile: much paler than adult, with a gray bill and same white rump patch

Nest: cup; female and male build; 1 brood per year

Eggs: 9-12; pinkish buff with brown markings

Incubation: 21-25 days; female and male incubate

Fledging: 49-52 days; female and male feed young

Migration: complete, to southern states and Central America

Food: insects, aquatic plants

Compare: Smaller than most waterfowl, it is the only black water bird or duck-like bird with a white bill.

Stan's Notes: An excellent diver and swimmer, often seen in large flocks on open water. Not a duck, as it has large lobed toes instead of webbed feet. When taking off, scrambles across surface of water with wings flapping. Bobs head while swimming. Floating nests are anchored to vegetation. Huge flocks of up to 1,000 birds gather for fall migration and during winter. The unusual name is of unknown origin, but in Middle English, *coote* was used to describe various waterfowl–perhaps it stuck. Also called Mud Hen.

13

YEAR-ROUND

AMERICAN CROW
Corvus brachyrhynchos

Size: 18" (45 cm)

Male: All-black bird with black bill, legs and feet. Can have purple sheen in direct sunlight.

Female: same as male

Juvenile: same as adult

Nest: platform; female builds; 1 brood per year

Eggs: 4-6; bluish to olive green, brown markings

Incubation: 18 days; female incubates

Fledging: 28-35 days; female and male feed young

Migration: non-migrator to partial migrator

Food: fruit, insects, mammals, fish, carrion, will come to seed and suet feeders

Compare: Similar to the Common Raven (rarely seen in Indiana), but has a smaller bill and lacks shaggy throat feathers. Crow has a higher pitched call than Raven's deep, low raspy call. Crow has a squared tail. Raven has a wedge-shaped tail, apparent in flight.

Stan's Notes: One of the most recognizable birds in Indiana. Often reuse nest every year if not taken over by a Great Horned Owl. They collect and store bright, shiny objects in the nest. Able to mimic human voices, and other birds. One of the smartest of all birds, they are very social, often entertaining themselves by provoking chases with other birds. They feed on road kill but are rarely hit by cars. Can live up to 20 years. Unmated birds, known as helpers, help raise young. Large extended families roost together at night, then disperse during the day to hunt.

15

soaring

TURKEY VULTURE
Cathartes aura

Size: 26-32" (66-80 cm); up to 6-foot wingspan

Male: Large bird with obvious red head and legs. When seen overhead, wings appear two-toned, black leading edge with gray on trailing edge and tip. Tip of wings end in finger-like projections. Squared-off tail. Ivory bill.

Female: same as male

Juvenile: same as adult, but often has a gray-to-blackish head and bill

Nest: no nest, or minimal nest on cliff or in cave; 1 brood per year

Eggs: 2; white with brown markings

Incubation: 38-41 days; female and male incubate

Fledging: 66-88 days; female and male feed young

Migration: complete, to southern states, Central and South Americas

Food: carrion, parents regurgitate for young

Compare: Smaller than the Bald Eagle (pg. 47), look for Vulture's two-toned colored wings. Flies holding wings in a slight V shape, unlike the straight wing position of the Eagle.

Stan's Notes: Vultures' naked heads are an adaptation to reduce the risk of feather fouling (picking up diseases) from carcasses. Unlike hawks and eagles, they have weak feet more suited to walking than grasping. One of the few birds with a developed sense of smell. They're generally mute, making only grunts or groans. Groups often seen in trees with wings outstretched to catch sun.

in flight

juvenile

crests

drying

DOUBLE-CRESTED CORMORANT
Phalacrocorax auritus

Size: 33" (84 cm); up to 4⅓-foot wingspan

Male: A large black water bird with a long snake-like neck. Two crests on head. Long gray bill with yellow at the base and a hooked tip.

Female: same as male

Juvenile: lighter brown with a grayish chest and neck

Nest: platform, in colony; male and female build; 1 brood per year

Eggs: 3-4; bluish white without markings

Incubation: 25-29 days; female and male incubate

Fledging: 37-42 days; male and female feed young

Migration: complete, to southern states, Mexico and Central America

Food: small fish, aquatic insects

Compare: Turkey Vulture (pg. 17) is similar in size and also perches on branches with wings open to dry in sun, but it has a naked red head. American Coot (pg. 13) lacks the long neck and long pointed bill.

Stan's Notes: Often seen flying in large V formation. Usually roosts in large groups in trees close to water. Catches fish by swimming underwater with wings held at its sides. Lacks the oil gland that keeps feathers from becoming waterlogged. To dry off it strikes an erect pose with wings outstretched, facing the sun. Common name refers to the two crests on its head, which are not usually seen. "Cormorant" comes from the Latin words *corvus,* meaning "crow," and *L. marinus*, meaning "pertaining to the sea," literally, "Sea Crow."

19

BLACK-AND-WHITE WARBLER
Mniotilta varia

Size: 5" (13 cm)

Male: Striped like a zebra, this small warbler has a white belly and black chin with distinctive black-and-white stripes on crown and black cheek patch.

Female: same as male, only duller and without the black chin and cheek patch

Juvenile: similar to female

Nest: cup; female builds; 1 brood per year

Eggs: 4-5; white with brown markings

Incubation: 10-11 days; female incubates

Fledging: 9-12 days; female and male feed young

Migration: complete, to Central and South Americas

Food: insects

Compare: Watch for Black-and-white Warbler creeping down a tree trunk, like White-breasted Nuthatch (pg. 177). The Brown Creeper (pg. 65) is brown and white with a white chest and belly. Creeper's bill is longer and curved downward.

Stan's Notes: One of the first warblers to return each spring. Look for this common warbler searching for insect eggs in the bark of large trees. The female will perform a distraction dance to draw predators away from nest. It is the only warbler that moves head-first down a tree trunk. Song sounds like a slowly turning, squeaky wheel. Makes nest on the ground concealed under dead leaves.

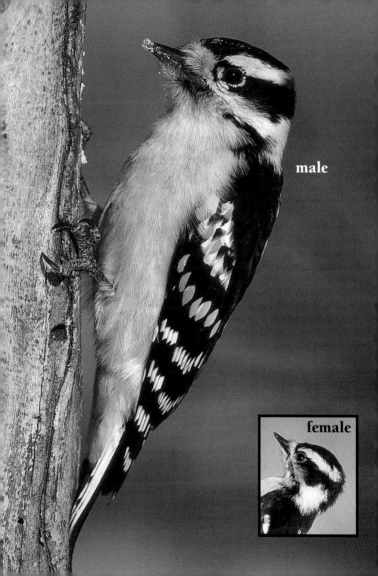

male

female

DOWNY WOODPECKER
Picoides pubescens

YEAR-ROUND

Size: 6" (15 cm)

Male: A small woodpecker with all-white belly, black-and-white spotted wings, a black line running through its eyes, a short black bill, a white stripe down back and a red mark on nape of neck. Several small black spots along side of white tail.

Female: same as male, lacking red mark on nape

Juvenile: same as female, some juveniles can have a red mark near forehead

Nest: cavity; male and female excavate cavity; 1 brood per year

Eggs: 3-5; white, unmarked

Incubation: 11-12 days; female and male incubate, female during day, male at night

Fledging: 20-25 days; male and female feed young

Migration: non-migrator

Food: insects, will come to seed and suet feeders

Compare: Almost identical to the Hairy Woodpecker (pg. 29), but smaller. Look for the shorter, thinner bill of Downy to differentiate them.

Stan's Notes: Both sexes will drum on a hollow log or branch to announce territories. Males perform most brooding and incubate all night. One of the most abundant woodpeckers. Small percentage of young will have a red spot on crown. Stiff tail feathers help brace the bird, like a tripod, as it clings to a tree branch. All woodpeckers have long barbed tongues, used to pull insects out of tiny places. Will winter roost in cavity.

female pg. 105

male

ROSE-BREASTED GROSBEAK
Pheucticus ludovicianus

MIGRATION
SUMMER

Size: 7-8" (18-20 cm)

Male: Plump black-and-white bird with large, triangular rose patch on center of chest. Wing linings are rosy red. Large ivory bill.

Female: heavily streaked brown and white with large white eyebrow line, wing linings are orange yellow

Juvenile: same as female

Nest: cup; female and male build; 1-2 broods per year

Eggs: 3-5; blue green with brown markings

Incubation: 13-14 days; female and male incubate

Fledging: 9-12 days; female and male feed young

Migration: complete, to Mexico, Central and South Americas

Food: insects, seeds, fruit, comes to seed feeders

Compare: Males are very distinctive with no look-alikes. Females look like large sparrows. Female is larger and has more distinctive eyebrow mark than female Purple Finch (pg. 85). Female House Finch (pg. 71) has no eyebrow mark.

Stan's Notes: Both males and females sing, but males sing much louder and clearer. Rich robin-like song. White wing patches flash when in flight. The name "Grosbeak" refers to its large bill, used to crush seeds. Male's red breast patch varies in size and shape in each individual. Males arrive first in spring, joined by females several days later. Late to arrive in spring and early to leave in autumn.

male

female

YELLOW-BELLIED SAPSUCKER
Sphyrapicus varius

MIGRATION
WINTER

Size: 8-9" (20-22.5 cm)

Male: Medium-sized woodpecker with checkered back. Has a red forehead, crown and chin. Tan-to-yellow chest and belly. White wing patches flash while flying.

Female: similar to male, white marking on chin

Juvenile: similar to adult, dull brown and lacks any red marking

Nest: cavity; female and male excavate; 1 brood per year

Eggs: 5-6; white, unmarked

Incubation: 12-13 days; female and male incubate, female during day, male at night

Fledging: 25-29 days; female and male feed young

Migration: complete, to Mexico and Central America

Food: insects, tree sap

Compare: Similar to other woodpeckers, but the male is the only Indiana woodpecker with a red chin patch. Female has white chin.

Stan's Notes: Drills holes in a pattern of horizontal rows in small- to medium-sized trees to bleed tree sap. Many birds drink from sapsucker taps. Oozing sap also attracts insects, which the sapsucker eats. Sapsuckers will defend their sapping sites from other birds. They don't suck sap; rather, they lap it with their long tongues. A quiet bird with few vocalizations, but will mew like a cat. Unlike other woodpeckers, drumming rhythm is irregular.

male

female

HAIRY WOODPECKER
Picoides villosus

YEAR-ROUND

Size: 9" (22.5 cm)

Male: Black-and-white woodpecker with a white belly and black wings with rows of white spots. White stripe down back. Long black bill. Red mark on back of head.

Female: same as male, lacks red spot

Juvenile: grayer version of adult, lacks red spot

Nest: cavity; female and male excavate hole; 1 brood per year

Eggs: 3-6; white, unmarked

Incubation: 11-15 days; female and male incubate, female during day, male at night

Fledging: 28-30 days; male and female feed young

Migration: non-migrator

Food: insects, seeds, nuts, will come to seed and suet feeders

Compare: Larger than Downy Woodpecker (pg. 23), Hairy has a longer bill and lacks Downy's black spots along tail.

Stan's Notes: A common backyard bird that announces its arrival with a sharp chirp before landing on feeders. Has tiny bristle-like feathers at base of bill to protect nostrils from wood dust. Barbed tongue helps extract insects from trees. Drums on hollow logs, branches or stovepipes in spring to announce territory. Responsible for eating many destructive forest insects. Often prefers to excavate nest cavities in live aspen trees. Has a large, more oval-shaped cavity entrance than that of Downy Woodpecker.

YEAR-ROUND

RED-HEADED WOODPECKER
Melanerpes erythrocephalus

Size: 9" (22.5 cm)

Male: All-red head and solid black back. White rump, chest and belly. Has large white patches on wings that flash when in flight. Black tail. Gray legs and bill.

Female: same as male

Juvenile: gray brown with white chest, lacking any red

Nest: cavity; male builds with help from female; 1 brood per year

Eggs: 4-5; white, unmarked

Incubation: 12-13 days; female and male incubate

Fledging: 27-30 days; female and male feed young

Migration: partial migrator, moves around to areas with abundant supply of nuts

Food: insects, fruit, nuts, comes to seed and suet feeders

Compare: No other Indiana woodpecker has an all-red head. Pileated Woodpecker (pg. 39) is the only other woodpecker with a solid black back, but has a partial red head.

Stan's Notes: Bill is not as well adapted for excavating holes as in other woodpeckers, so it chooses dead or rotten tree branches for nest. Later nesting than the closely related Red-bellied Woodpecker and will often take over its nest cavity. Prefers more open or edge woodland with many dead trees. Often seen perching on tops of dead snags. Stores acorns and other nuts.

male

female

RED-BELLIED WOODPECKER
Melanerpes carolinus

YEAR-ROUND

Size: 9¼" (23 cm)

Male: "Zebra-backed" woodpecker with a white rump. Red crown extends down the nape of neck. Tan breast with a tinge of red on belly, which is often hard to see.

Female: same as male, with gray crown

Juvenile: gray version of adult, no red crown or nape

Nest: cavity; female and male build; 1 brood per year

Eggs: 4-5; white, unmarked

Incubation: 12-14 days; female and male incubate, female during day, male at night

Fledging: 24-27 days; female and male feed young

Migration: non-migrator

Food: insects, nuts, fruit, will come to seed and suet feeders

Compare: Similar to Northern Flicker (pg. 125) and Yellow-bellied Sapsucker (pg. 27). Note tan chest and belly with obvious stripes on back. The Red-headed Woodpecker (pg. 31) has an all-red head.

Stan's Notes: Mostly a bird of shady woodland, it excavates holes in rotten wood looking for spiders, centipedes and beetles. Often kicked out of nest hole by European Starlings. Will return to same tree to excavate a new nest below that of previous year. Hammers acorns and berries into crevices of trees for winter food.

female pg. 135

male

MIGRATION

LESSER SCAUP
Aythya affinis

Size: 16-17" (40-43 cm)

Male: Appears mostly black with bold white sides and gray back. Chest and head look nearly black but in sun, head appears purple with green highlights. Bright yellow eye.

Female: overall brown with a dull white patch near base of bill

Juvenile: same as female

Nest: ground; female builds; 1 brood per year

Eggs: 8-14; olive buff without markings

Incubation: 22-28 days; female incubates

Fledging: 45-50 days; female teaches young to feed

Migration: complete, to the southern states, northern South America and Central America

Food: aquatic plants and insects

Compare: Male Blue-winged Teal (pg. 133) is smaller and has a bright white crescent-shaped patch near base of bill.

Stan's Notes: Probably one of the most common of all the diving ducks in Indiana. Often seen in large flocks numbering in the thousands on area lakes, ponds and sewage lagoons. Usually only seen during spring and fall migrations. When observed in flight, note the bold white stripe under the wings. Has an interesting baby-sitting arrangement in which the young form groups tended by one to three adult females.

female pg. 141

male

YEAR-ROUND
SUMMER

HOODED MERGANSER
Lophodytes cucullatus

Size: 16-19" (40-48 cm)

Male: A sleek black-and-white bird with rusty brown sides. Crest "hood" raises to reveal large white patch. Long, thin black bill.

Female: sleek brown and rust bird with a ragged rusty crest and long, thin brown bill

Juvenile: similar to female

Nest: cavity; female lines former woodpecker hole; 1 brood per year

Eggs: 10-12; white, unmarked

Incubation: 32-33 days; female incubates

Fledging: 71 days; female feeds young

Migration: complete, to Gulf coast and Mexico

Food: small fish, aquatic insects

Compare: Smaller than the male Common Merganser (pg. 217). A distinctive diving bird, look for the male's large white patch on the head and rusty brown sides.

Stan's Notes: Not as common as the Common Merganser, the male Hooded Merganser can voluntarily raise and lower the crest on its head to show off the large white patch. Females will "dump" eggs into other female Hooded Mergansers' nests, resulting in 20 to 25 eggs in some nests. Mergansers have been known to share a nesting cavity with Common Goldeneyes and Wood Ducks sitting side by side.

male

female

PILEATED WOODPECKER
Dryocopus pileatus

YEAR-ROUND

Size: 19" (48 cm)

Male: Large, crow-sized black-backed woodpecker with bright red crest on head. Long gray bill with red mustache. Leading edge of wings white, flashing brightly when flying.

Female: same as male, but has a black forehead and lacks red mustache

Juvenile: similar to adult, only duller and browner overall

Nest: cavity; male and female excavate; 1 brood per year

Eggs: 3-5; white, unmarked

Incubation: 15-18 days; female and male incubate, female during day, male at night

Fledging: 26-28 days; female and male feed young

Migration: non-migrator

Food: insects, suet, will come to suet feeders

Compare: Red-headed Woodpecker (pg. 31) is about half the size, and has an all-red head, black back and white rump.

Stan's Notes: Our largest woodpecker, it excavates long oval holes up to several feet long in tree trunks, searching for insects. Large chips of wood lie at the base of excavated trees. Will drum on hollow branches, chimneys, etc., to announce its territory. Relatively shy bird that prefers large tracts of woodland. The young are fed regurgitated insects. Favorite food is carpenter ants.

male

female pg. 145

WINTER

COMMON GOLDENEYE
Bucephala clangula

Size: 18½-20" (47-50 cm)

Male: A mostly white duck with a black back, a large, puffy green head and a large white spot in front of each bright golden eye. Dark bill.

Female: brown and gray, a large dark brown head, gray body, white collar, bright golden eyes, yellow-tipped dark bill.

Juvenile: same as female, but has a dark bill

Nest: cavity; female lines former woodpecker cavity; 1 brood per year

Eggs: 8-10; light green without markings

Incubation: 28-32 days; female incubates

Fledging: 56-59 days; female leads young to food

Migration: complete, to southern states

Food: aquatic plants, insects

Compare: Similar to, but larger than, the black and white male Lesser Scaup (pg. 35). Look for distinctive white mark in front of its golden eye and white chest.

Stan's Notes: Known for their loud whistling, which is produced by their wings in flight. In late winter and early spring, males often attract females through elaborate displays, throwing their heads backwards while uttering a single raspy note. Females will lay eggs in other goldeneye nests, resulting in some mothers incubating up to 30 eggs. Received its common name from its obvious bright golden eyes.

soaring

OSPREY
Pandion haliaetus

MIGRATION

Size: 24" (60 cm); up to 6-foot wingspan

Male: Large eagle-like bird with white belly and black brown back. Large wings are angled (cocked) backwards with black "wrist" marks. White head with a black streak across eyes.

Female: same as male

Juvenile: same as adult

Nest: platform; female and male build; 1 brood per year

Eggs: 2-4; white with brown markings

Incubation: 32-42 days; female and male incubate

Fledging: 48-58 days; male and female feed young

Migration: complete, to Mexico, Central and South Americas

Food: fish

Compare: Bald Eagle (pg. 47) is on average ten inches larger, and has an all-white head and tail. Immature Bald Eagles are all brown with white speckles. Look for a white belly and dark stripe across eye to identify Osprey.

Stan's Notes: Ospreys are in a family all their own. It is the only raptor that will plunge into the water to catch fish. Look for its angulated wings while in flight. Nests on man-made towers and tall dead trees. Can hover for a few seconds before diving. Carries fish in a head-first position during flight for better aerodynamics. Recent studies show that male and female might mate for life, but don't migrate to the same wintering grounds.

43

COMMON LOON
Gavia immer

MIGRATION

Size: 28-36" (71-90 cm)

Male: Large, familiar black-and-white bird of the lakes. Checkerboard back with white necklace, black head and deep red eye. Long, pointed black bill in summer. Entirely gray body and bill in fall and winter.

Female: same as male

Juvenile: gray version of adult, without red eye

Nest: platform, on the ground; female and male build; 1 brood per year

Eggs: 2; olive brown, occasionally brown markings

Incubation: 26-31 days; female and male incubate

Fledging: 75-80 days; female and male feed young

Migration: complete, to Gulf coast, southern states and Mexico

Food: fish, aquatic insects

Compare: Double-crested Cormorant (pg. 19) has a black chest and gray bill with yellow at the base and a hooked tip.

Stan's Notes: A true symbol of the wildness of our lakes. Prefers clear lakes because it hunts for fish by eyesight. Legs are set so far back that it has a hard time walking on land, but it's a great swimmer. Its name comes from the Swedish word *lom*, meaning "lame," for the awkward way it walks on land. Its unique call suggests the wild laughter of a demented person, and led to the phrase "crazy as a loon." Young ride on the backs of swimming parents. Adults will perform distraction displays to protect young. Very sensitive to disturbance during nesting and will abandon nest.

45

soaring

juvenile

BALD EAGLE
Haliaeetus leucocephalus

Size: 31-37" (79-94 cm); up to 7-foot wingspan

Male: Dark brown-to-black body and wings set off by a pure white head and tail. Large, curved yellow bill and yellow feet.

Female: same as male, only slightly larger

Juvenile: dark brown with white spots or speckles throughout its body and wings, gray bill

Nest: massive platform; female and male build; 1 brood per year

Eggs: 2; off-white, unmarked

Incubation: 34-36 days; female and male incubate

Fledging: 75-90 days; female and male feed young

Migration: partial migrator to southeastern states

Food: fish, carrion, ducks

Compare: Larger than the Turkey Vulture (pg. 17). Mature Bald Eagle has white head and tail. Turkey Vulture has two-toned wings and flies with its wings in a V shape, unlike the straight-out wing position of the Eagle.

Stan's Notes: Often seen soaring, this bird is making a comeback in Indiana. Juveniles attain white head and tail at about 4 to 5 years of age. For their midair mating ritual, one bird flips upside down, locking talons with another. Both tumble until they break apart to continue flying. Bald Eagle returns to the same nest every year, adding sticks, enlarging it to massive proportions, at times up to 1,000 pounds. Thought to mate for life, but will switch mates if not successful reproducing.

SUMMER

TREE SWALLOW
Tachycineta bicolor

Size: 5-6" (13-15 cm)

Male: Blue green in spring and greener in fall. Appears to change color in direct sunlight. White belly, a notched tail and pointed wing tips.

Female: similar to male, duller

Juvenile: gray brown with white belly and grayish breast band

Nest: cavity; female and male line former woodpecker cavity or nest box; 1 brood per year

Eggs: 4-6; white, unmarked

Incubation: 13-16 days; female incubates

Fledging: 20-24 days; female and male feed young

Migration: complete, to Mexico and Central America

Food: insects

Compare: Similar color to Purple Martin (pg. 57), but smaller and has white chest and belly. Barn Swallow (pg. 53) has rust belly and deeply forked tail.

Stan's Notes: The first swallow to return each spring. Easily attracted to your yard with a nest box. Competes with Eastern Bluebirds for nest boxes. Travels great distances to find dropped feathers to line its grass nest. Sometimes seen playing by chasing after dropped feathers. Often seen flying back and forth across open fields, feeding on insects. Gathers in large flocks to migrate.

female pg. 83

male

INDIGO BUNTING
Passerina cyanea

Size: 5½" (14 cm)

Male: Vibrant blue finch-like bird. Scattered dark markings on wings and tail.

Female: light brown bird with faint markings

Juvenile: similar to female

Nest: cup; female builds; 2 broods per year

Eggs: 3-4; pale blue, unmarked

Incubation: 12-13 days; female incubates

Fledging: 10-11 days; female feeds young

Migration: complete, to Mexico, Central America and South America

Food: insects, seeds, fruit, will visit seed feeders

Compare: Smaller than Eastern Bluebird (pg. 55) and lacking Bluebird's red chest patch.

Stan's Notes: Usually only the males are noticed. Actually a black bird, as it doesn't have any blue pigment in its feathers. As with Blue Jays, the sunlight is refracted within the structure of the bunting's feathers, making them appear blue. Appears iridescent in direct sunlight. Molts to acquire body feathers with gray tips, which quickly wear off to reveal bright blue plumage. Males often sing from treetops to attract mates. Will come to feeders in spring before insects are plentiful. Mostly seen along woodland edges, feeding on insects. Migrates at night in flocks of five to ten birds. A late migrant, with males returning before females and juveniles. Males nearly always return to previous year's nest site. Juveniles move to within a mile from birth site.

SUMMER

BARN SWALLOW
Hirundo rustica

Size: 7" (18 cm)

Male: A sleek swallow with a blue black back, cinnamon belly and reddish brown chin. White spots on long forked tail.

Female: same as male, only slightly duller

Juvenile: similar to adult, with tan belly and chin and shorter tail

Nest: cup; female and male build; 2 broods per year

Eggs: 4-5; white with brown markings

Incubation: 13-17 days; female incubates

Fledging: 18-23 days; female and male feed young

Migration: complete, to South America

Food: insects, prefers beetles, wasps and flies

Compare: Tree Swallow (pg. 49) has white belly and chin, and notched tail. The Chimney Swift (pg. 67) has narrow pointed tail with wings longer than body. Purple Martin (pg. 57) is nearly two inches larger and has a dark purple belly.

Stan's Notes: Of the six swallow species in Indiana, this is the only one with a deeply forked tail. Unlike other swallows, the Barn Swallow rarely glides in flight, so look for continuous flapping. It builds mud nests using up to 1,000 beak-loads of mud, often in or on barns. Nests in colonies of four to six, but nesting alone is not uncommon. They drink while flying by skimming water or getting water from wet leaves. They also bathe while flying through rain or sprinklers.

male

female

EASTERN BLUEBIRD
Sialia sialis

Size: 7" (18 cm)

Male: Reminiscent of its larger cousin, American Robin, with a rusty red breast and white belly. Sky blue head, back and tail.

Female: shares rusty red breast and white belly, but is grayer with faint blue tail and wings

Juvenile: similar to female, with spots on chest, blue wing markings

Nest: cavity, old woodpecker cavity or man-made nest box; female builds; 2 broods per year

Eggs: 4-5; pale blue, unmarked

Incubation: 12-14 days; female incubates

Fledging: 15-18 days; male and female feed young

Migration: complete, to southern states

Food: insects, fruit

Compare: Male Indigo Bunting (pg. 51) is nearly all blue, lacking rusty red chest. The Blue Jay (pg. 59) is considerably larger with a crest and white markings.

Stan's Notes: A year-round resident in southern Indiana, the Eastern Bluebird population sometimes drops due to unseasonably cold and wet weather in spring. Although a permanent resident, some Eastern Bluebirds migrate each spring and autumn. Bluebirds like open fields, pastures, roadsides and other open habitats. Perches on tree or fence post and waits for grasshoppers and other insects. Young of first brood will help raise young of second. Gathers in large family groups for migration and during winter.

male

female

SUMMER

PURPLE MARTIN
Progne subis

Size: 8½" (22 cm)

Male: A large swallow-shaped bird with purple head, back and belly. Black wings and tail. Notched tail.

Female: gray purple head and back with a whitish belly, darker wings and tail

Juvenile: same as female

Nest: cavity; female and male line cavity of house; 1 brood per year

Eggs: 4-5; white, unmarked

Incubation: 15-18 days; female incubates

Fledging: 26-30 days; male and female feed young

Migration: complete, to South America

Food: insects

Compare: The male is the only dark-purple-bellied swallow. Usually only seen in groups.

Stan's Notes: The largest swallows in North America. Formerly nested in tree cavities, but now nearly exclusively nest in man-made nest boxes in Indiana. Their main diet consists of dragonflies, not mosquitoes as once thought. Often drink and bathe while flying by skimming water or flying through rain. Return to same nest site each year. Males arrive before females and yearlings. Often nest within 100 feet of a human dwelling, and in fact, the most successful colonies are located within this distance. Young strike out to form new colonies. Huge colonies gather in autumn to migrate to South America.

YEAR-ROUND

BLUE JAY
Cyanocitta cristata

Size: 12" (30 cm)

Male: A large bright light blue and white bird with a black necklace. Crest on head moves up and down at will. Gray belly with white face. White wing bars on blue wing. Blue tail with black spots and white tip.

Female: same as male

Juvenile: same as adult, only duller

Nest: cup; female and male build; 1-2 broods per year

Eggs: 4-5; green to blue with brown markings

Incubation: 16-18 days; female incubates

Fledging: 17-21 days; female and male feed young

Migration: non-migrator to partial migrator, moves around to find abundant food source

Food: insects, fruit, carrion, seeds, nuts, attracted to seed feeders

Compare: Eastern Bluebird (pg. 55) is much smaller and lacks the crest. The Belted Kingfisher (pg. 61) lacks vivid blue color and black necklace of the Blue Jay.

Stan's Notes: One of the few birds to cache food. Will scream like a hawk to scatter birds at a feeder before approaching. Feathers don't have blue pigment; refracted sunlight casts blue light. Known as the alarm of the forest, screaming at any intruders in the woods. Is known to eat eggs or young birds from the nests of other birds.

male

female

BELTED KINGFISHER
Ceryle alcyon

YEAR-ROUND

Size: 13" (33 cm)

Male: Large blue gray bird with white belly. Broad blue gray breast band and a ragged crest that can be raised and lowered at will. Large head with long thick black bill. Small white spot directly in front of red brown eye. Wing tips black with splashes of white that flash when flying.

Female: same as male, but has an additional rusty breast band and flank

Juvenile: same as adult

Nest: cavity; female and male excavate; 1 brood per year

Eggs: 6-7; white, unmarked

Incubation: 23-24 days; female and male incubate

Fledging: 23-24 days; female and male feed young

Migration: complete, to southern states, Central and South Americas

Food: small fish

Compare: Similar in size to the Blue Jay (pg. 59), but Kingfisher is darker blue with larger, more ragged crest.

Stan's Notes: Seen perched on branches near water, it dives head-first for small fish and returns to a branch to eat. Has a loud machine-gun-like call. Excavates a deep cavity in bank of river or lake. Parents drop dead fish into water, teaching young to dive. Regurgitates pellets of bone after meals, being unable to pass bones through digestive tract. Mates recognize each other by call.

CHESTNUT-SIDED WARBLER
Dendroica pensylvanica

Size: 5" (13 cm)

Male: A colorful combination of a yellow cap and black mask set against a white face, chin, chest and belly. Two yellow wing bars. Chestnut-colored flanks. Gray wings.

Female: similar to male, but flanks duller brown

Juvenile: similar to female, lime green head and back, white eye ring and bright yellow wing bars, lacks chestnut sides

Nest: cup; female builds; 1 brood per year

Eggs: 3-5; white with brown markings

Incubation: 12-13 days; female incubates

Fledging: 10-12 days; female and male feed young

Migration: complete, to Central America

Food: insects, berries

Compare: Shares yellow cap with the Yellow-rumped Warbler (pg. 173), but lacks yellow sides and rump. The Yellow Warbler (pg. 255) is nearly all yellow and lacks the Chestnut's white chest and chestnut-colored flanks.

Stan's Notes: Prefers young, open aspen forest. Look for this attractive warbler in the spring, hopping high in the branches while it hunts for insects. You will usually only get a glimpse of this fast-moving warbler. Will hold its tail in an uplifted position, showing white tail. Not uncommon for this bird to approach humans in defense of a nest site.

YEAR-ROUND

BROWN CREEPER
Certhia americana

Size: 5" (13 cm)

Male: A small, thin, nearly camouflaged bird with white belly, long stiff tail and thin curved bill. Obvious white line above dark eye.

Female: same as male

Juvenile: same as adult

Nest: cup; female builds; unknown how many broods per year

Eggs: 5-6; white with tiny brown markings

Incubation: 14-17 days; female incubates, male feeds female during incubation

Fledging: 13-16 days; female and male feed young

Migration: partial migrator

Food: insects, nuts, seeds

Compare: Creeps up tree trunks, not down, like the White-breasted Nuthatch (pg. 177). Watch for Creeper to fly from the top of one trunk to the bottom of another, working its way to the top, looking for insects. Slightly larger than the Red-breasted Nuthatch (pg. 167), with a similar white mark above eye, but Creeper has a white belly, long tail and no black crown.

Stan's Notes: Utilizes camouflage coloring to defend itself by spreading out flat on a branch or trunk without moving. The young are able to follow parents, creeping soon after fledging. Commonly seen in wooded areas. Often builds nest behind loose bark of dead or dying trees.

SUMMER

CHIMNEY SWIFT
Chaetura pelagica

Size: 5" (13 cm)

Male: A nondescript, all-brown swallow-shaped bird, usually only seen flying. Long thin body with pointed tail and head. Long swept-back wings are longer than body.

Female: same as male

Juvenile: same as adult

Nest: half cup; female and male build; 1 brood per year

Eggs: 4-5; white, unmarked

Incubation: 19-21 days; female and male incubate

Fledging: 28-30 days; female and male feed young

Migration: complete, to South America

Food: insects

Compare: Considerably smaller than Purple Martin (pg. 57) and lacks Martin's iridescent purple color. Barn Swallow (pg. 53) has forked tail, compared with the pointed tail of the Chimney Swift. Tree Swallow (pg. 49) has white belly and blue green back.

Stan's Notes: Often called Flying Cigar due to its pointed body shape. Spends all day flying, rarely perching. They bathe and drink by skimming across water surfaces. Hundreds nest and roost in large chimneys, hence the common name. One of the fastest flyers in the bird world. Unique in-flight twittering call is often heard before bird is seen. Fly in groups, feeding on flying insects nearly 100 feet in the air. Nest, made of tiny twigs, is cemented with saliva and attached to inside of chimneys or hollow trees.

SUMMER

CHIPPING SPARROW
Spizella passerina

Size: 5" (13 cm)

Male: A small gray brown sparrow with a clear gray chest, rusty crown, white eyebrow with a black eye line, a thin gray black bill and two faint wing bars.

Female: same as male

Juvenile: similar to adult, but has streaked chest and lacks rusty cap

Nest: cup; female builds; 2 broods per year

Eggs: 3-5; blue green with brown markings

Incubation: 11-14 days; female incubates

Fledging: 10-12 days; female and male feed young

Migration: complete, to southern states, Central America and Mexico

Food: insects, seeds, will come to ground feeders

Compare: Similar to American Tree Sparrow (pg. 87), which shares the rusty crown, but lacks the dark eye stripe. Look for clear gray chest of Chipping Sparrow. Two inches smaller than the rusty Fox Sparrow (pg. 95).

Stan's Notes: Common garden or yard bird often seen feeding below feeders on dropped seeds. Gathers in large family groups to feed each autumn in preparation for migration. Nest is placed low in dense shrubs and is almost always lined with animal hair. Often just called Chippy. Received its common name from the male's fast "chip" call. Migrates at night in flocks of 20 to 30 birds.

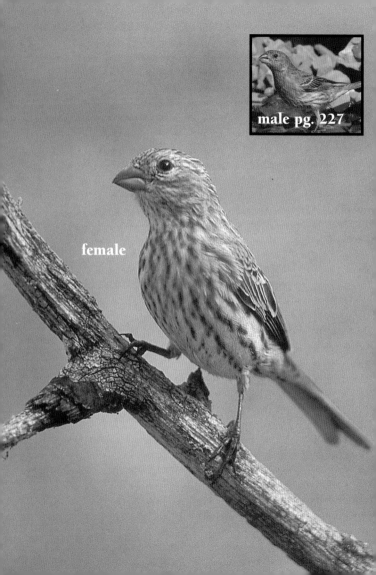

male pg. 227

female

HOUSE FINCH
Carpodacus mexicanus

YEAR-ROUND

Size: 5" (13 cm)

Female: A plain brown bird with a heavily streaked white chest.

Male: orange red face, chest and rump, with a dark brown marking behind eye, brown wings streaked with white, white belly with brown streaks, brown cap

Juvenile: similar to female

Nest: cup, sometimes in cavities; female builds; 2 broods per year

Eggs: 4-5; pale blue, lightly marked

Incubation: 12-14 days; female incubates

Fledging: 15-19 days; female and male feed young

Migration: non-migrator to partial migrator, moves around to find food

Food: seeds, fruit, leaf buds, will come to seed feeders

Compare: Very similar to female Purple Finch (pg. 85). Lacking Purple Finch's bold white eyebrow. The female American Goldfinch (pg. 249) has a clear chest and white wing bars. Very similar to Pine Siskin (pg. 75), but without Siskin's yellow wing bars.

Stan's Notes: A relatively new bird to Indiana (first reported in 1976), it was originally introduced to Long Island, New York, in the 1940s from western America. A very social bird, it visits feeders in small flocks. Seems to prefer nesting in hanging flower baskets. Incubating female is fed by male. Loud and cheerful warbling song.

SUMMER

HOUSE WREN
Troglodytes aedon

Size: 5" (13 cm)

Male: A small all-brown bird with light brown marking on tail and wings. Brown, slightly curved bill. Often holds its tail erect.

Female: same as male

Juvenile: same as adult

Nest: cavity; female and male line just about any cavity; 2 broods per year

Eggs: 4-6; tan with brown markings

Incubation: 10-13 days; female and male incubate

Fledging: 12-15 days; female and male feed young

Migration: complete, to southern states and Mexico

Food: insects

Compare: Distinguished from Carolina Wren (pg. 77) by the lack of brow marking.

Stan's Notes: Prolific songsters, they sing from dawn to dusk during mating season. Easily attracted to nesting boxes. In spring, the male chooses several prospective nesting cavities and places a few small twigs in each. Female inspects each, chooses one, and finishes the nest building. She will completely fill nest cavity with uniformly small twigs, then line a small depression at back of cavity with pine needles and grass. Often has trouble fitting long twigs through nest cavity hole. Tries many different directions and approaches until successful.

WINTER

PINE SISKIN
Carduelis pinus

Size: 5" (13 cm)

Male: Small brown finch. Heavily streaked back, breast and belly. Yellow wing bars. Yellow at the base of tail. Thin bill.

Female: similar to male, with less yellow

Juvenile: similar to adult, light yellow tinge over the breast and chin

Nest: modified cup; female builds; 2 broods

Eggs: 3-4; greenish blue with brown markings

Incubation: 12-13 days; female incubates

Fledging: 14-15 days; female and male feed young

Migration: irruptive; moves around the United States in search of food

Food: seeds, insects; will come to seed feeders

Compare: Female American Goldfinch (pg. 249) lacks streaks and has white wing bars. Female House Finch (pg. 71) has a streaked chest, but lacks yellow wing bars. Female Purple Finch (pg. 85) has bold white eyebrows.

Stan's Notes: Usually considered a winter finch, this bird can be seen in flocks of up to 20 individuals and is often seen with Evening Grosbeaks. More common in the northern half of Indiana, but can be found throughout the state in heavy invasion years; it is absent from Indiana in some winters. Will come to thistle feeders. Travels and breeds in small groups, with nests often only a few feet apart. Males feed females during incubation. Juveniles lose yellow tint of chest and chin by late summer of their first year.

75

CAROLINA WREN
Thryothorus ludovicianus

YEAR-ROUND

Size: 5½" (14 cm)

Male: Warm rusty brown head and back with an orange yellow chest and belly. White throat and a prominent white eye stripe. Short stubby tail often cocked up.

Female: same as male

Juvenile: same as adult

Nest: cavity; female and male build; 2 broods per year, sometimes 3

Eggs: 4-6; white, sometimes pink or creamy, with brown markings

Incubation: 12-14 days; female incubates

Fledging: 12-14 days; female and male feed young

Migration: non-migrator

Food: insects, fruit, few seeds

Compare: Similar to the House Wren (pg. 73), but the Carolina Wren has the prominent white eyebrow. Look for the stubby upturned tail.

Stan's Notes: Mates are long-term, remaining together throughout the year in permanent territories. Will sing throughout the year. The male is known to sing up to 40 different song types, singing one song repeatedly before switching to another. Females also sing, resulting in duets. Male often takes over feeding first brood of young while the female renests. Range expands northward in years with mild winters. Will nest in birdhouses or in the most unusual places, such as mailboxes, bumpers of cars, broken taillights or just about any other cavity. Found in woodland or brushy yards.

SONG SPARROW
Melospiza melodia

Size: 5-6" (13-15 cm)

Male: Common brown sparrow with heavy dark streaks on chest coalescing into a central dark spot.

Female: same as male

Juvenile: similar to adult, finely streaked chest without central spot

Nest: cup; female builds; 2 broods per year

Eggs: 3-4; pale blue to green with reddish brown marks

Incubation: 12-14 days; female incubates

Fledging: 9-12 days; female and male feed young

Migration: complete, to southern states

Food: insects, seeds, rarely visits seed feeders

Compare: Similar to other brown sparrows, look for heavily streaked chest with central dark spot.

Stan's Notes: Many Song Sparrow subspecies or varieties, but central dark spot carries through each variant. While the female builds another nest for second brood, the male often takes over feeding the young. Returns to similar area each year, defending its small territory by singing from thick shrubs. Common host of Brown-headed Cowbird. Ground feeders, look for them to scratch simultaneously with both feet to expose seeds. Unlike many sparrow species, Song Sparrows rarely flock together.

male pg. 175

female

WINTER

DARK-EYED JUNCO
Junco hyemalis

Size: 5½" (14 cm)

Female: A round bird with a tan-to-brown chest, head and back. White belly, ivory-to-pink bill and dark eye. Since the outermost tail feathers are white, tail appears as a white V in flight.

Male: same as female, only slate gray to charcoal

Juvenile: similar to female, with streaked chest and head

Nest: cup; female and male build; 2 broods per year

Eggs: 3-5; white with reddish brown markings

Incubation: 12-13 days; female incubates

Fledging: 10-13 days; male and female feed young

Migration: complete, all across United States

Food: seeds, insects, will come to seed feeders

Compare: Rarely confused with other birds. Large flocks come to feed under bird feeders.

Stan's Notes: One of Indiana's most common winter birds. Usually seen on the ground in small flocks. Migrates from Canada to Indiana and beyond. Females tend to migrate farther south than males. Look for white outer tail feathers that flash in flight. Several species of juncos have now been combined into one, simply called Dark-eyed Junco. Most comfortable on the ground, juncos "double-scratch" with both feet to expose seeds and insects. Consume many weed seeds. A flocking bird, it adheres to a rigid social hierarchy with dominant birds chasing less dominant birds.

female

male pg. 51

INDIGO BUNTING
Passerina cyanea

SUMMER

Size: 5½" (14 cm)

Female: A light brown finch-like bird with faint streaking on light tan chest. Wings have very faint blue cast with indistinct wing bars.

Male: vibrant blue finch-like bird, scattered dark markings on wings and tail

Juvenile: similar to female

Nest: cup; female builds; 2 broods per year

Eggs: 3-4; pale blue, unmarked

Incubation: 12-13 days; female incubates

Fledging: 10-11 days; female feeds young

Migration: complete, to Mexico, Central America and South America

Food: insects, seeds, fruit, will visit seed feeders

Compare: Similar to female finches. Female American Goldfinch (pg. 249) has white wing bars. Female Purple Finch (pg. 85) has a heavily streaked chest and white eye lines. Female House Finch (pg. 71) also has heavily streaked chest.

Stan's Notes: A secretive bird, usually only the males are seen. Males often sing from treetops to attract mates. Will come to feeders in spring before insects are plentiful. Mostly seen along woodland edges, feeding on insects. Migrates at night in flocks of five to ten birds. A late migrant, with males returning before females and juveniles. Juveniles move to within a mile from birth site.

male pg. 229

female

WINTER

PURPLE FINCH
Carpodacus purpureus

Size: 6" (15 cm)

Female: A plain brown bird with a heavily streaked chest. Prominent white eye line.

Male: raspberry red head, cap, breast, back and rump, brownish wings and tail

Juvenile: same as female

Nest: cup; female and male build; 1 brood per year

Eggs: 4-5; greenish blue with brown markings

Incubation: 12-13 days; female incubates

Fledging: 13-14 days; female and male feed young

Migration: irruptive, moves around the state to find food

Food: seeds, insects, fruit, will come to seed feeders

Compare: The female House Finch (pg. 71) lacks white eyebrow. The Pine Siskin (pg. 75) has yellow wing bars. The female American Goldfinch (pg. 249) has a clear chest and white wing bars.

Stan's Notes: Usually only seen during winter, when flocks of Purple Finches leave their northern homes and move around looking for food. Travels in flocks of up to 50. Comes to seed feeders along with House Finches, making it hard to tell them apart. A rich loud song and a distinctive "tic" note is made only in flight. Not a purple color, the Latin name *purpureus* means "crimson" or other reddish color.

side view

front view

WINTER

AMERICAN TREE SPARROW
Spizella arborea

Size: 6" (15 cm)

Male: A common brown sparrow with tan breast and rusty crown. Note single black spot in center of breast. Upper bill dark, lower bill yellow. Two white wing bars. Gray eyebrow.

Female: same as male

Juvenile: lacking rusty crown, has a streaked chest often obscuring the central dark spot

Nest: cup; female builds; 1 brood per year

Eggs: 3-5; green white with brown markings

Incubation: 12-13 days; female incubates

Fledging: 8-10 days; female and male feed young

Migration: complete, throughout North America

Food: insects, seeds, occasionally comes to feeders

Compare: Looks similar to other sparrows, so look closely for the single dark spot in the center of the breast. Shares a rusty crown with the Chipping Sparrow (pg. 69), but lacks Chippy's distinctive white eyebrow and black eye line. Song Sparrow (pg. 79) has a heavily streaked chest.

Stan's Notes: A regular winter bird feeder visitor throughout the state. Also seen during spring and fall migrations in small flocks of 2 to 200. Sometimes called Winter Chippy since it looks similar to Chipping Sparrow, a summer visitor. Nests in northern Canada.

male

female

HOUSE SPARROW
Passer domesticus

YEAR-ROUND

Size: 6" (15 cm)

Male: Medium sparrow-like bird with large black spot on chin extending down to the chest. Brown back with white wing bar. A gray belly and crown.

Female: all-light-brown bird, lacking black throat patch and wing bar, slightly smaller

Juvenile: similar to female

Nest: domed cup nest, within cavity; female and male build; 2-3 broods per year

Eggs: 4-6; white with brown markings

Incubation: 10-12 days; female incubates

Fledging: 14-17 days; female and male feed young

Migration: non-migrator, moves around to find food

Food: seeds, insects, fruit, comes to seed feeders

Compare: Lacks the rusty crown of American Tree Sparrow (pg. 87) and Chipping Sparrow (pg. 69). Look for male House Sparrow's black bib. Female has clear chest and no marking on head (cap).

Stan's Notes: Introduced from Europe to Central Park, New York, in 1850 and now found throughout North America. These birds are not really sparrows, but members of the Weaver Finch family, characterized by large, oversized domed nests. Constructs a nest containing scraps of plastic, paper and whatever else is available. Aggressive bird that will kill the young of other birds in order to take over a cavity. Familiar city bird, nearly always in flocks.

WHITE-THROATED SPARROW
Zonotrichia albicollis

Size: 6-7" (15-18 cm)

Male: A brown sparrow with gray tan chest and belly. Small yellow spot between the eyes, called lore. Distinctive white throat patch. Crown has white or tan stripes alternating with black stripes.

Female: same as male

Juvenile: brown version of adult, eyebrow and throat gray with heavily streaked chest

Nest: cup; female builds; 1 brood per year

Eggs: 4-6; varies between greenish, bluish and creamy white, with red brown markings

Incubation: 11-14 days; female incubates

Fledging: 10-12 days; female and male feed young

Migration: complete, to southern states and Mexico

Food: insects, fruit, seeds, will come to ground feeders

Compare: The White-crowned Sparrow (pg. 93) has a black-and-white striped crown, without the yellow lore or white throat patch.

Stan's Notes: There are two color variations (polymorphic) of White-throated Sparrows: tan-striped and white-striped. Studies indicate the white-striped adults tend to mate with the tan-striped birds. No indication why. Nests are built on the ground under small trees in bogs and coniferous forests.

juvenile

WINTER

WHITE-CROWNED SPARROW
Zonotrichia leucophrys

Size: 6½-7½" (16-19 cm)

Male: A brown sparrow with gray chest and a black-and-white striped crown. Small thin pink bill.

Female: same as male

Juvenile: similar to adult, with brown stripes on head instead of white

Nest: cup; female builds; 2 broods per year

Eggs: 3-5; varies between greenish, bluish and whitish, with red brown markings

Incubation: 11-14 days; female incubates

Fledging: 8-12 days; male and female feed young

Migration: complete, to southern states and Mexico

Food: insects, seeds, berries, will come to ground feeders

Compare: The White-throated Sparrow (pg. 91) has white- or tan-striped crown, white throat patch, and yellow spot between eyes and bill, with a blackish bill.

Stan's Notes: Doesn't nest in Indiana. Males take most of the responsibility of raising young while female starts a second brood. Only 9 to 12 days separate the broods. Feeds on the ground by scratching backwards with both feet at the same time. Usually seen in groups of up to 20 during spring and fall migrations.

FOX SPARROW
Passerella iliaca

MIGRATION
WINTER

Size: 7" (18 cm)

Male: A plump rusty-red sparrow with a heavily streaked, rust-colored breast and solid rust tail. Head and back are mottled with gray.

Female: same as male

Juvenile: same as adult

Nest: cup; female builds; 2 broods per year

Eggs: 2-4; pale green with reddish markings

Incubation: 12-14 days; female incubates

Fledging: 10-11 days; female and male feed young

Migration: complete, to southern states

Food: insects, seeds, comes to feeders

Compare: Similar coloration as the Brown Thrasher (pg. 119), but the Fox Sparrow is smaller, plumper and has a smaller bill. Rusty color differentiates it from all other sparrows.

Stan's Notes: One of the largest sparrows, it is often only seen under seed feeders during spring and autumn migrations. Scratches like a chicken with both feet at the same time to find seeds and insects. Nests on the ground in brush and forest edges in Canada. The name "Sparrow" comes from the Anglo-Saxon word *spearwa*, which means "flutterer," as applied to any small bird. "Fox" refers to the bird's rusty color.

95

female

male
pg. 3

EASTERN TOWHEE
Pipilo erythrophthalmus

YEAR-ROUND
SUMMER

Size: 7-8" (18-20 cm)

Female: A mostly light brown bird with rusty red brown sides and white belly. Long brown tail with white tip. Short, stout, pointed bill with rich red eye. White wing patches flash in flight.

Male: similar to female, but is black, not brown

Juvenile: light brown, heavily streaked head, chest and belly, long dark tail with white tip

Nest: cup; female builds; 2 broods per year

Eggs: 3-4; creamy white with brown markings

Incubation: 12-13 days; female incubates

Fledging: 10-12 days; female and male feed young

Migration: complete, to southern states and South America

Food: insects, seeds, fruit, comes to ground feeder

Compare: Slightly smaller than the American Robin (pg. 191). Female Rose-breasted Grosbeak (pg. 105) has a heavily streaked chest and white eye mark.

Stan's Notes: Common name comes from its distinctive "tow-hee" call given by both sexes. Mostly known for its characteristic call that sounds like, "Drink-your-tea!" White-eyed form in southern states. Seen hopping backward with both feet to rake up leaf litter, called bilateral scratching, in search of insects and seeds. Female broods, but male does most of the feeding of young.

1 year old

Bohemian
Waxwing

YEAR-ROUND

CEDAR WAXWING
Bombycilla cedrorum

Size: 7½" (19 cm)

Male: A very sleek-looking brown gray bird with a pointed crest on head, light yellow belly and bandit-like black mask. The tip of its tail is bright yellow and the tips of its wings look as if they have been dipped in red wax.

Female: same as male

Juvenile: grayish with a heavily streaked chest, lacks red wing tips, black mask and sleek look

Nest: cup; female and male build; 1 brood per year, occasionally 2

Eggs: 4-6; pale blue with brown markings

Incubation: 10-12 days; female incubates

Fledging: 14-18 days; female and male feed young

Migration: partial migrator

Food: fruit, insects

Compare: Similar to its larger, less common cousin, Bohemian Waxwing (see inset), which has white on wings and rust under tail. Female Cardinal (pg. 109) has large red bill.

Stan's Notes: The name is derived from their red wax-like wing tips and preference for eating small blueberry-like cones of the cedar. Mostly seen in flocks, moving from area to area, looking for berries. More often seen in winter only because naked branches reveal their presence. Spends most of its time at the tops of tall trees. In summer, before berries are abundant, they feed on insects. Listen for the very high-pitched whistling sounds that the birds constantly make. Wanders in winter to find available food supplies. Obtains mask after first year.

male pg. 5

female

YEAR-ROUND

BROWN-HEADED COWBIRD
Molothrus ater

Size: 7½" (19 cm)

Female: Dull brown gray bird without any obvious markings. Pointed, sharp gray bill.

Male: glossy black bird with chocolate brown head

Juvenile: similar to female, only duller gray with streaked chest

Nest: no nest; lays eggs in nests of other birds

Eggs: 5-7; white with brown markings

Incubation: 10-13 days; host bird incubates eggs

Fledging: 10-11 days; host birds feed young

Migration: complete, to southern states

Food: insects, seeds, will come to seed feeders

Compare: In the blackbird family. The slightly larger female Red-winged Blackbird (pg. 111) has a white eye line and a streaked chest. The European Starling (pg. 7) has speckles, a long, pointed yellow bill and short tail.

Stan's Notes: Of about 750 species of parasitic birds worldwide, this is the only parasitic bird in Indiana, laying all eggs in host birds' nests, leaving others to raise its young. Cowbirds are known to have laid eggs in nests of over 200 species of birds. Some birds reject cowbird eggs, but most raise them, even to the exclusion of their own young. Look for warblers and other birds feeding young birds twice their own size. At one time they followed bison to feed on the insects attracted to the animals.

HORNED LARK
Eremophila alpestris

Size: 7-8" (18-20 cm)

Male: A sleek tan-to-brown bird. Black necklace with yellow chin and black bill. Two tiny "horns" on top of the head, which can be difficult to see. Black tail with white outer feathers noticeable in flight.

Female: same as male, only duller, "horns" less noticeable

Juvenile: lacks all black markings and yellow chin, doesn't form "horns" until second year

Nest: ground; female builds; 2 broods per year

Eggs: 3-4; gray with brown markings

Incubation: 11-12 days; female incubates

Fledging: 9-12 days; female and male feed young

Migration: non-migrator to partial migrator in Indiana

Food: seeds, insects

Compare: Larger than the House Sparrow (pg. 89). Look for a black mark on Horned Lark's face and neck.

Stan's Notes: The "Lark" name comes from the Middle English word *laverock*, or "a lark." Larks are birds of open ground. The only true lark in North America. A very common bird in rural areas. Almost always seen in large flocks along country roads. Some pairs have up to three broods per year because they get such an early start. Females perform a fluttering distraction display if nest is disturbed. Females can renest about seven days after brood fledges. Population increased over the past 100 years due to clearing land for farming.

female

male
pg. 25

ROSE-BREASTED GROSBEAK
Pheucticus ludovicianus

MIGRATION
SUMMER

Size: 7-8" (18-20 cm)

Female: Plump, heavily streaked brown and white bird with obvious white eyebrow line. Wing linings are orange yellow.

Male: plump black-and-white bird with large, triangular rose patch on center of chest, wing linings are rosy red, large ivory bill

Juvenile: same as female

Nest: cup; female and male build; 1-2 broods per year

Eggs: 3-5; blue green with brown markings

Incubation: 13-14 days; female and male incubate

Fledging: 9-12 days; female and male feed young

Migration: complete, to Mexico, Central and South Americas

Food: insects, seeds, fruit, comes to seed feeders

Compare: Females look like large sparrows. Female is larger and has more distinctive eyebrow mark than female Purple Finch (pg. 85). Female House Finch (pg. 71) has no eyebrow mark. Males are very distinctive with no look-alikes.

Stan's Notes: Both females and males sing, but males sing much louder and clearer. Rich robin-like song. White wing patches flash when in flight. The name "Grosbeak" refers to its large bill, used to crush seeds. Male's red breast patch varies in size and shape in each individual. Males arrive first in spring, joined by females several days later. Late to arrive in spring and early to leave in autumn.

winter

breeding

SPOTTED SANDPIPER
Actitis macularius

SUMMER

Size: 8" (20 cm)

Male: Olive brown back and a white chest with black spots. White line over eye and short bill with long dull yellow legs. Lacks breast spots in fall and winter.

Female: same as male

Juvenile: similar to adult, lacking spots on chest and darker bill

Nest: ground; female and male build; 2 broods per year

Eggs: 3-4; brownish with brown markings

Incubation: 20-24 days; male incubates

Fledging: 17-21 days; male feeds young

Migration: complete, southern states and South America

Food: aquatic insects

Compare: Much smaller than the Greater Yellowlegs (pg. 131) and Lesser Yellowlegs (pg. 117). Look for Spotted Sandpiper's black spots extending from chest down to abdomen.

Stan's Notes: One of the more common sandpipers, females mate with multiple males and lay eggs in up to five different nests. Males incubate and care for young. Constantly bobs tail while standing and walks as if delicately balanced. Flies with wings held in cup-like arc, never really lifted above a horizontal plane. Able to fly straight up out of the water. One of the few shorebirds that will actually dive underwater if pursued. When this bird is in winter plumage, it lacks spots.

male pg. 233

female

juvenile

YEAR-ROUND

NORTHERN CARDINAL
Cardinalis cardinalis

Size: 8-9" (20-22.5 cm)

Female: Buff brown bird with tinges of red on crest and wings, a black mask and large red bill.

Male: red bird with a black mask extending from face down to chin and throat, large red bill and crest

Juvenile: same as female, with blackish gray bill

Nest: cup; female builds; 2-3 broods per year

Eggs: 3-4; bluish white with brown markings

Incubation: 12-13 days; female and male incubate

Fledging: 9-10 days; female and male feed young

Migration: non-migrator

Food: seeds, insects, fruit, will come to seed feeders

Compare: Female Cardinal appears similar to juvenile Cardinal. Look for female's bright red bill.

Stan's Notes: A familiar backyard bird, look for male feeding female during courtship. Male feeds young of first brood by himself while female builds second nest. Their name comes from the Latin word *cardinalis*, which means "important." Very territorial during spring, it will fight its own reflection in a window. Non-territorial in winter, they gather in small flocks of up to 20 birds. Both male and female sing, and can be heard anytime of year. Listen for their "whata-cheer-cheer-cheer" territorial call in spring.

male pg. 9

female

YEAR-ROUND

RED-WINGED BLACKBIRD
Agelaius phoeniceus

Size: 8½" (22 cm)

Female: A heavily streaked brown bird with white eyebrow and pointed brown bill.

Male: jet black bird with red and yellow patch on upper wing, pointed black bill

Juvenile: same as female

Nest: cup; female builds; 2-3 broods per year

Eggs: 3-4; bluish green with brown markings

Incubation: 10-12 days; female incubates

Fledging: 11-14 days; female and male feed young

Migration: complete, to southern states, Mexico and Central America

Food: insects, seeds, will come to seed feeders

Compare: Slightly larger than female Brown-headed Cowbird (pg. 101), which lacks white eyebrow and streaks on chest. Similar to the female Rose-breasted Grosbeak (pg. 105), only thinner body and long pointed bill.

Stan's Notes: It is a sure sign of spring when the Red-winged Blackbirds return to the marsh. Flocks of up to 100,000 birds have been reported. Males return before females and defend territories. Will repeat call from top of cattail while showing off red and yellow wing bars, called epaulets. Females choose mate. Nests are usually over shallow water in thick stand of cattails. One of the most widespread and numerous birds in Indiana. Feeds mostly on seeds in spring and fall, switching to insects during summer.

in flight

SUMMER

COMMON NIGHTHAWK
Chordeiles minor

Size: 9" (22.5 cm)

Male: A camouflaged brown and white bird with white chin. Distinctive white bands across wings and tail seen only in flight.

Female: similar to male, but with tan chin and lacking white tail band

Juvenile: same as adult

Nest: no nest; lays eggs on the ground, usually on rocks, or on rooftop; 1 brood per year

Eggs: 2; cream with lavender markings

Incubation: 19-20 days; female and male incubate

Fledging: 20-21 days; female and male feed young

Migration: complete, to South America

Food: insects caught in air

Compare: Much larger than Chimney Swift (pg. 67). Look for the obvious white wing bars of Common Nighthawk.

Stan's Notes: Usually only seen flying at dusk or after sunset, but not uncommon during the day. Prolific insect eater. One of the first birds to migrate each autumn. More common in the city than country. Prefers gravel rooftops for nesting. Very noisy birds, repeating a "peenting" call during flight. Alternates slow wing beats with bursts of quick wing beats. Males' distinctive springtime mating ritual is a steep diving flight terminated with a loud popping noise.

male

female

NORTHERN BOBWHITE
Colinus virginianus

Size: 10" (25 cm)

Male: A short, stocky, mostly brown bird with a short gray tail. A prominent white eye stripe and white throat. Reddish brown sides and belly, often with black lines and dots.

Female: similar to male, but has a buff brown eye stripe and throat

Juvenile: smaller and duller than adult

Nest: ground; female and male build; 1 brood per year

Eggs: 12-15; white to creamy, unmarked

Incubation: 23-24 days; female and male incubate

Fledging: 6-7 days; female and male feed young

Migration: non-migrator

Food: insects, seeds, fruit, will come to ground feeders offering corn and millet

Compare: Smaller than female Ring-necked Pheasant (pg. 159) and lacks Pheasant's long tail.

Stan's Notes: Moves around in small flocks of 20 birds (often family members), called a covey. The covey often rests together at night, in a tight circle with tails together and heads facing outward to watch for predators. Both males and females perform a distraction display if the nest or young are threatened. Male gives a rising whistle, "bob-white," heard mainly in spring and summer. Also gives a single "hoy" call year-round. Prefers shrubs, orchards, hedgerows and pastures. Nest is nothing more than a depression in the ground lined with grass. Often pulls nearby vegetation over the nest to help conceal it.

LESSER YELLOWLEGS
Tringa flavipes

Size: 10-11" (25-28 cm)

Male: Typical sandpiper-type bird with brown back and wings, and lightly streaked white breast and belly. Thin, straight black bill and long yellow legs.

Female: same as male

Juvenile: same as adult

Nest: ground; female builds; 1 brood per year

Eggs: 3-4; yellowish with brown markings

Incubation: 22-23 days; male and female incubate

Fledging: 18-20 days; male and female lead young to food

Migration: complete, to South America

Food: aquatic insects

Compare: Nearly a carbon copy of Greater Yellowlegs (pg. 131), only smaller with shorter bill.

Stan's Notes: Usually seen in large flocks, they comb shorelines and mud flats looking for aquatic insects. They use their long straight bills to pluck insects and tiny fish from water. Very shy bird that quite often moves into the water prior to taking flight. Has a variety of "flight" notes that it gives when taking off. A member of the group of sandpipers called Tattlers, all of which scream alarm calls when taking flight. Most often seen in head down, tail up position, walking along, looking to snatch up something to eat. Nests on marshes in spruce forests of central Alaska and central Canada. Nest is a simple depression atop a mound of earth. Migrates later than Greater Yellowlegs in spring and earlier in fall.

BROWN THRASHER
Toxostoma rufum

YEAR-ROUND
SUMMER

Size: 11" (28 cm)

Male: A rusty red bird with long tail and heavily streaked chest and belly. Two white wing bars. Long curved bill and bright yellow eye.

Female: same as male

Juvenile: same as adult, eye color grayish

Nest: cup; female and male build; 2 broods per year

Eggs: 4-5; pale blue with brown markings

Incubation: 11-14 days; female and male incubate

Fledging: 10-13 days; female and male feed young

Migration: complete, to southern states

Food: insects, fruit

Compare: Slightly larger in size and similar in shape to the American Robin (pg. 191) and Gray Catbird (pg. 187), but the Thrasher has a streaked chest and rusty color. Similar rusty color as Fox Sparrow (pg. 95), but Brown Thrasher is larger and thinner.

Stan's Notes: Prodigious songsters, they are often found in thick shrubs where they sing deliberate musical phrases, repeating each twice. The male has the largest documented song repertoire of all North American birds, with over 1,100 song types. Often seen quickly flying in and out of thick or dense shrubs.

KILLDEER
Charadrius vociferus

Size: 11" (28 cm)

Male: An upland shorebird that has 2 black bands around the neck like a necklace. A brown back and white belly. Bright reddish orange rump, visible in flight.

Female: same as male

Juvenile: similar to adult, with 1 neck band

Nest: ground; male builds; 2 broods per year

Eggs: 3-5; tan with brown markings

Incubation: 24-28 days; male and female incubate

Fledging: 25 days; male and female lead their young to food

Migration: complete, to southern states, Mexico and Central America

Food: insects

Compare: The Spotted Sandpiper (pg. 107) is found around water and lacks the 2 neck bands of the Killdeer.

YEAR-ROUND
WINTER

Stan's Notes: The only shorebird with two black neck bands. It is known for its broken wing impression, which draws intruders away from nest. Once clear of the nest, the Killdeer takes flight. Nests are only a slight depression in a gravel area, often very difficult to see. Young look like miniature adults on stilts when first hatched. Able to follow parents and peck for insects soon after birth. Technically classified as a shorebird, but doesn't live at the shore. Often seen in vacant fields or by railroads. Migrates in small flocks. Gives a very distinctive "kill-deer" call.

AMERICAN KESTREL
Falco sparverius

Size: 10-12" (25-30 cm)

Male: Rusty brown back and tail. White chest with dark spots. Double black vertical lines on white face. Males have blue gray wings. Distinctive wide black band with white edge on tip of rusty tail.

Female: similar to male, slightly larger, but with rusty brown wings and dark bands on tail

Juvenile: same as adult

Nest: cavity; doesn't build nest within; 1 brood per year

Eggs: 4-5; white with brown markings

Incubation: 29-31 days; male and female incubate

Fledging: 30-31 days; female and male feed young

Migration: complete, to southern states and Central America, small percentage non-migrator

Food: insects, small mammals and birds, reptiles

Compare: Similar to other falcons. Look for the two vertical black stripes on face of Kestrel. No other small bird of prey has rusty-colored back or tail.

Stan's Notes: Formerly called Sparrow Hawk due to its small size. Seen hovering near roads before diving for prey. Adapts quickly to a wooden nest box. Has pointed swept-back wings seen in flight. Perches nearly upright. Kestrels are rare raptors in that the males and females have quite different markings. Watch for them to pump their tails up and down after landing on perches.

123

female

male

NORTHERN FLICKER
Colaptes auratus

YEAR-ROUND

Size: 12" (30 cm)

Male: Brown and black woodpecker with a large white rump patch visible only when flying. Black necklace above a speckled breast. Red spot on nape of neck and black mustache.

Female: same as male, lacking black mustache

Juvenile: same as adult

Nest: cavity; female and male excavate; 1 brood per year

Eggs: 5-8; white, unmarked

Incubation: 11-14 days; female and male incubate

Fledging: 25-28 days; female and male feed young

Migration: complete, to southern states

Food: insects, especially ants

Compare: Yellow-bellied Sapsucker (pg. 27) is smaller, and has red chin and forehead. Red-bellied Woodpecker (pg. 33) has a black-and-white zebra-striped back, red patch on head and lacks mustache. Flickers are the only brown-backed woodpeckers in Indiana.

Stan's Notes: The flicker is the only woodpecker to regularly feed on the ground, preferring ants and beetles. Produces an antacid saliva to neutralize the acidic defense of ants. Males usually select nest site, which takes up to 12 days to excavate. Flashes golden yellow under wings and tail in flight. Undulates deeply in flight while giving a loud "wacka-wacka" call.

MOURNING DOVE
Zenaida macroura

YEAR-ROUND

Size: 12" (30 cm)

Male: Smooth fawn-colored dove with black spots on wings and tail. Single black spot behind and below eye. Pointed wedge-shaped tail with white edges. Gray patch on the head. Iridescent pink, green around neck.

Female: similar to male, lacks iridescent neck feathers

Juvenile: spotted and streaked, called a squab

Nest: platform; female and male build; 2 broods per year

Eggs: 2; white, unmarked

Incubation: 13-14 days; male and female incubate, male during day, female at night

Fledging: 12-14 days; female and male feed young

Migration: partial migrator, moves around to find food, or to southern states

Food: seeds, will come to seed feeders

Compare: Smaller than Rock Pigeon (pg. 197), lacking its wide range of color combinations.

Stan's Notes: Name comes from its mournful cooing. A ground feeder, bobbing its head as it walks. One of the few birds to drink without lifting head, same as Rock Pigeon. Parents feed their young (squab) a regurgitated liquid called crop-milk for the first few days of life. Flimsy platform nest of twigs often falls apart in a storm. Wind rushing through wing feathers in flight creates characteristic whistling sound.

PIED-BILLED GREBE
Podilymbus podiceps

Size: 13" (33 cm)

Male: Small brown water bird with a black chin and black ring around a thick, chicken-like ivory bill. Puffy white patch under tail. Has an unmarked brown bill during winter.

Female: same as male

Juvenile: paler than adult, with white spots and gray chest, belly and bill

Nest: floating platform; female and male build; 1 brood per year

Eggs: 5-7; bluish white, unmarked

Incubation: 22-24 days; female and male incubate

Fledging: 22-24 days; female and male feed young

Migration: complete, to southern states, Mexico and Central America

Food: aquatic insects, fish

Compare: The smallest brown water bird that dives underwater for long periods of time.

Stan's Notes: A very common water bird. Often seen diving for crayfish, aquatic insects and fish. It slowly sinks like a submarine when disturbed. Formerly called Hell-diver because of the length of time it stays submerged. Can surface far away from where it went under. Builds a platform nest on a floating mat in water. Particularly sensitive to pollution. Adapted well to life on the water, with short wings, lobed toes and legs set close to rear of body. While swimming is easy, they are very awkward on land. The name "Grebe" probably came from the Old English word *krib*, meaning "crest," a reference to the Great Crested Grebe found in Europe.

GREATER YELLOWLEGS
Tringa melanoleuca

Size: 14" (36 cm)

Male: A tall bird with bulbous head and long thin bill, slightly turned up. Gray streaking on chest and white belly. Long yellow legs.

Female: same as male

Juvenile: same as adult

Nest: ground; female builds; 1 brood per year

Eggs: 3-4; off-white with brown markings

Incubation: 22-23 days; female and male incubate

Fledging: 18-20 days; male and female feed young

Migration: complete, to southern states and South America

Food: small fish, aquatic insects

Compare: Nearly identical to the Lesser Yellowlegs (pg. 117), but larger, and with a longer and upturned bill.

Stan's Notes: A common shorebird identified by slightly upturned bill and long yellow legs, often seen resting on one leg. Its long legs carry it through deep water. Nests on the ground near water on the northern tundra of Labrador and Newfoundland. Often seen feeding by rushing forward through the water, plowing its bill or swinging it from side to side, catching small insects or fish. A skittish bird quick to give an alarm call, causing flocks to take flight. Quite often moves into the water prior to taking flight. Has a variety of "flight" notes that it gives when taking off.

female

male

BLUE-WINGED TEAL
Anas discors

Size: 15-16" (38-40 cm)

Male: Small, plain-looking brown duck speckled with black. Gray head with a large white crescent-shaped mark at base of bill. Black tail with small white patch. Blue wing patch usually seen only in flight.

Female: duller version of male, lacking facial crescent mark and white tail markings

Juvenile: same as female

Nest: ground; female builds; 1 brood per year

Eggs: 8-11; creamy white

Incubation: 23-27 days; female incubates

Fledging: 35-44 days; female feeds young

Migration: complete, southern states, Central America

Food: aquatic plants, seeds, aquatic insects

Compare: Nearly half the size of the female Mallard (pg. 157). The female Blue-winged Teal is similar to the female Wood Duck (pg. 143), but lacks the Wood Duck's bright white eye ring and crest.

Stan's Notes: Males leave females near end of incubation. Females will perform distraction displays to protect nests and young. Blue wing patch is called a speculum. Nest is built some distance from water. Planting crops and cultivating to pond edges are causing a decline in population.

male pg. 35

female

MIGRATION

LESSER SCAUP
Aythya affinis

Size: 16-17" (40-43 cm)

Female: An overall brown duck with a white patch at base of a light gray bill.

Male: white and gray, the chest and head appear nearly black; in direct sun, head appears purple with green highlights

Juvenile: same as female

Nest: ground; female builds; 1 brood per year

Eggs: 8-14; olive buff without markings

Incubation: 22-28 days; female incubates

Fledging: 45-50 days; female teaches young to feed

Migration: complete, to the southern states, northern South America and Central America

Food: aquatic plants and insects

Compare: Male Blue-winged Teal (pg. 133) is smaller and has a bright white crescent-shaped patch near base of bill.

Stan's Notes: Probably one of the most common of all the diving ducks in Indiana. Often seen in large flocks numbering in the thousands on area lakes, ponds and sewage lagoons. Usually only seen during spring and fall migrations. When observed in flight, note the bold white stripe under the wings. Has an interesting baby-sitting arrangement in which the young form groups tended by one to three adult females.

soaring

BROAD-WINGED HAWK
Buteo platypterus

SUMMER

Size: 14-19" (36-48 cm)

Male: A hawk slightly smaller than the American Crow, the Broad-winged has a brown back and rusty red barring on chest. Tail has two or three wide black-and-white bands. White under wings, with black "fingertips" when seen in flight.

Female: same as male

Juvenile: tail bands narrower and more numerous, brown-streaked chest and belly

Nest: platform; female and male build, but female finishes; 1 brood per year

Eggs: 2-3; off-white with brown markings

Incubation: 28-32 days; female incubates, male feeds female during incubation

Fledging: 34-35 days; female and male feed young

Migration: complete, to Central and South Americas

Food: small mammals, small birds, large insects, snakes, frogs

Compare: Similar in size to Cooper's Hawk (pg. 199), but with wider, shorter tail. Larger than Sharp-shinned Hawk (pg. 195). Note alternating white and black tail bands.

Stan's Notes: A very common hawk in Indiana. Often seen in large groups (kettles) migrating early in autumn. Massive migration provides a spectacular sight along the Great Lakes coastline. Spends most of its time hunting snakes, small birds and frogs in dense woodland. Short round wings propel it through dense woods.

137

RUFFED GROUSE
Bonasa umbellus

Size: 16-19" (40-48 cm)

Male: A brown chicken-like bird with a long squared tail. Wide black band near tip of tail, is able to fan tail like a turkey. Tuft of feathers on head stands like a crown. Black ruffs on sides of neck.

Female: same as male, but less obvious neck ruffs

Juvenile: same as female

Nest: ground; female builds, 1 brood per year

Eggs: 9-12; tan with light brown markings

Incubation: 23-24 days; female incubates

Fledging: 10-12 days; female leads young to food

Migration: non-migrator

Food: seeds, insects, fruit, leaf buds

Compare: Female Ring-necked Pheasant (pg. 159), is larger with a longer, pointed tail. Look for a feathered tuft on the head and black ruffs on the neck of the Ruffed Grouse.

YEAR-ROUND

Stan's Notes: A common bird of deep woods. Often seen in aspen or other trees, feeding on leaf buds. Female will perform distraction display to protect young. Grows bristles on its feet in winter to serve as snowshoes. If there is enough snow, it will dive into a snowbank to roost at night. In spring, male raises crest (tuft), fans tail feathers, and stands on logs and drums with wings to attract females. Drumming sound comes from cupped wings moving air, not pounding on chest or log. Two color types, red and gray, most apparent in the tail. Black ruffs around the neck gave rise to its common name.

139

female

male pg. 37

HOODED MERGANSER
Lophodytes cucullatus

YEAR-ROUND
SUMMER

Size: 16-19" (40-48 cm)

Female: Sleek brown and rust bird with a red head. Ragged "hair" on back of head. Long, thin brown bill.

Male: same size and shape as female, but black back and rust sides, crest "hood" raises to reveal large white patch, long black bill

Juvenile: similar to female

Nest: cavity; female lines former woodpecker hole; 1 brood per year

Eggs: 10-12; white, unmarked

Incubation: 32-33 days; female incubates

Fledging: 71 days; female feeds young

Migration: complete, to Gulf coast and Mexico

Food: small fish, aquatic insects

Compare: Smaller than female Common Merganser (pg. 235) and lacking white chest.

Stan's Notes: Not as common as the Common Merganser, the male Hooded Merganser can voluntarily raise and lower the crest on its head to show off the large white patch. Females will "dump" eggs into other female Hooded Mergansers' nests, resulting in 20 to 25 eggs in some nests. Mergansers have been known to share a nesting cavity with Common Goldeneyes and Wood Ducks sitting side by side.

141

male pg. 211

female

WOOD DUCK
Aix sponsa

YEAR-ROUND
SUMMER

Size: 17-20" (43-50 cm)

Female: A small brown dabbling duck. Bright white eye ring and not so obvious crest. Blue patch on wing is often hidden.

Male: highly ornamented with a green head and crest, red eye, patterned with white and black, rusty chest and white belly

Juvenile: same as female

Nest: cavity; female lines former woodpecker cavity; 1 brood per year

Eggs: 10-15; creamy white, unmarked

Incubation: 28-36 days; female incubates

Fledging: 56-68 days; female teaches young to feed

Migration: complete, to southern states

Food: aquatic insects, plants, seeds

Compare: Smaller than the female Northern Shoveler (pg. 147) and lacks the long wide bill. Smaller than the female Mallard (pg. 157), which lacks Wood Duck's white eye ring.

Stan's Notes: A common duck of quiet, shallow backwater ponds. Nests in old woodpecker holes or nest boxes. Often seen flying deep within a forest or perched high up on branches of trees. Female takes flight with loud squealing call and enters nest cavity from full flight. Will lay eggs in neighboring female nest, called egg dumping, resulting in some clutches in excess of 20 eggs. Young remain in nest cavity only 24 hours after hatching, then jump from up to 30 feet to the ground or water to follow their mother. After that, they never return to the nest.

143

female

male pg. 41

COMMON GOLDENEYE
Bucephala clangula

Size: 18½-20" (47-50 cm)

Female: A brown and gray duck with a large dark brown head, gray body, a white·collar and bright golden eyes. Yellow-tipped dark bill.

Male: mostly white duck with black back, a large, puffy green head, with a large white spot in front of each bright golden eye, dark bill

Juvenile: same as female, but has a dark bill

Nest: cavity; female lines former woodpecker cavity; 1 brood per year

Eggs: 8-10; light green without markings

Incubation: 28-32 days; female incubates

Fledging: 56-59 days; female leads young to food

Migration: complete, to southern states

Food: aquatic plants, insects

Compare: Similar to, but larger than, the brown and white female Lesser Scaup (pg. 135). Look for female Goldeneye's dark brown head and white collar.

Stan's Notes: Known for their loud whistling, which is produced by their wings in flight. In late winter and early spring, males often attract females through elaborate displays, throwing their heads backwards while uttering a single raspy note. Females will lay eggs in other goldeneye nests, resulting in some mothers incubating up to 30 eggs. Received its common name from its obvious bright golden eyes.

male pg. 215

female

NORTHERN SHOVELER
Anas clypeata

Size: 20" (50 cm)

Female: A medium-sized brown duck speckled with black. Green speculum. Has an extraordinarily large spoon-shaped bill, almost always held pointed towards the water.

Male: same spoon-shaped bill, iridescent green head, rusty sides and a white breast

Juvenile: same as female

Nest: ground; female builds; 1 brood per year

Eggs: 9-12; olive, unmarked

Incubation: 22-25 days; female incubates

Fledging: 30-60 days; female leads young to food

Migration: complete, to southern states and Central America

Food: aquatic insects, plants

Compare: Similar to female Mallard (pg. 157). Check for spoon-shaped bill. Larger than the average female Wood Duck (pg. 143), lacking white eye ring.

Stan's Notes: Seen in small flocks of five to ten, swimming low in water with large bills always pointed towards water, as if they're too heavy to lift. More commonly seen during spring migration. Feeds primarily by filtering tiny plants and insects from the water's surface with bill.

BARRED OWL
Strix varia

Size: 20-24" (50-60 cm)

Male: A chunky brown and gray owl with dark horizontal barring on chest, and vertical streaking on belly. Large head with dark brown eyes.

Female: same as male, only slightly larger

Juvenile: same as adult

Nest: cavity; no nesting material brought in; 1 brood per year

Eggs: 2-3; white, unmarked

Incubation: 28-33 days; female incubates

Fledging: 42-44 days; female and male feed young

Migration: non-migrator

Food: mammals, small birds

Compare: Lacks the "horns" of the Great Horned Owl (pg. 153). It's our only owl with dark eyes. About twice the size of the tiny Eastern Screech-Owl (pg. 189).

Stan's Notes: A very common owl that can often be seen hunting during the day. Prefers dense woodland with sparse undergrowth. Can be attracted with a simple nest box with a large opening attached to a tree. The young will stay with the parents for up to four months after fledging. Often sounds like a dog barking just before giving an eight-hoot call that sounds like, "Who-cooks-for-you? Who-cooks-for-you?" Great Horned Owl sounds like, "Hoo-hoo-hoo-hoooo!"

soaring

RED-TAILED HAWK
Buteo jamaicensis

YEAR-ROUND

Size: 19-25" (48-63 cm); up to 4-foot wingspan

Male: A large hawk with an amazing variety of colors from bird to bird, from chocolate brown to nearly all white. Often brown with white breast and distinctive brown belly band. Rust red tail usually only seen from above. Underside of wing white with small dark patch on leading edge near shoulder.

Female: same as male, often larger

Juvenile: similar to adult, lacking red tail, speckled chest

Nest: platform; male and female build; 1 brood per year

Eggs: 2-3; white, unmarked or occasionally marked with brown

Incubation: 30-35 days; female and male incubate

Fledging: 45-46 days; male and female feed young

Migration: partial migrator, to southern states, small percentage non-migrator

Food: mice, birds, snakes, insects

Compare: Nearly twice the size of the Sharp-shinned Hawk (pg. 195).

Stan's Notes: The most common hawk of open country and cities, often seen perched on freeway light posts. Look for it circling above open fields searching for prey. Will return to the same nest site each year. Doesn't develop red tail until second year.

151

YEAR-ROUND

GREAT HORNED OWL
Bubo virginianus

Size: 20-25" (50-63 cm)

Male: A robust brown "horned" owl with bright yellow eyes and V-shaped white bib.

Female: same as male, only slightly larger

Juvenile: similar to adult

Nest: no nest; takes over the nests of crows, Great Blue Herons and hawks, or uses partial cavities; 1 brood per year

Eggs: 2; white, unmarked

Incubation: 26-30 days; female incubates

Fledging: 30-35 days; male and female feed young

Migration: non-migrator

Food: small mammals, birds, snakes, insects

Compare: The Barred Owl (pg. 149) has no "horns" and dark eyes. Over twice the size of the Eastern Screech-Owl (pg. 189).

Stan's Notes: Earliest nesting bird in Indiana, it lays eggs in January and February. Has excellent hearing; able to hear a mouse moving under a foot of snow. "Ears" are actually tufts of feathers (horns) and have nothing to do with hearing. Not able to turn head all the way around. Wing feathers are ragged on the end, resulting in a silent flight. Eyelids close from the top down, like humans. Fearless, it is one of the few animals that will kill skunks and porcupines. Because of this, it is sometimes called Flying Tiger.

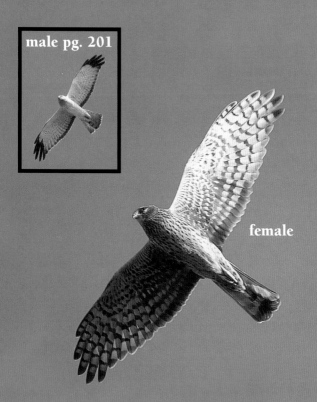

male pg. 201

female

NORTHERN HARRIER
Circus cyaneus

YEAR-ROUND

Size: 24" (60 cm)

Female: A slim, low-flying hawk. Dark brown back with brown-streaked breast and belly. Large white rump patch. Narrow black bands across tail. Tips of wings black.

Male: silver gray with large white rump patch and white belly, faint narrow bands across tail, tips of wings black

Juvenile: similar to female, with orange breast

Nest: platform; female and male build; 1 brood per year

Eggs: 4-8; bluish white, unmarked

Incubation: 31-32 days; female incubates

Fledging: 30-35 days; male and female feed young

Migration: complete, southern states, Central America

Food: mice, snakes

Compare: Slimmer than Red-tailed Hawk (pg. 151). Look for black bands on tail and a white rump patch.

Stan's Notes: One of the easiest hawks to identify. Harriers glide just above ground, following the contours of the land while searching for prey. Wings are held just above the horizontal position, tilting back and forth in the wind, similar to Turkey Vultures. Formerly called Marsh Hawk due to its habit of hunting over marshes. Nests on the ground. At all ages, the Northern Harrier has distinctive owl-like face disks.

male pg. 219

female

YEAR-ROUND

MALLARD
Anas platyrhynchos

Size: 27-28" (69-71 cm)

Female: All-brown duck with orange and black bill and small blue and white wing mark, called a speculum.

Male: large, bulbous green head, white necklace, rust brown or chestnut chest, combination of gray and white on sides, yellow bill, legs and feet

Juvenile: same as female, but with yellow bill

Nest: ground; female builds; 1 brood per year

Eggs: 7-10; greenish to whitish, unmarked

Incubation: 26-30 days; female incubates

Fledging: 42-52 days; female leads young to food

Migration: complete, to southern states, small percentage non-migrator

Food: seeds, plants, aquatic insects, ground feeders offering corn

Compare: The female Northern Shoveler (pg. 147) is smaller and has a large spoon-shaped bill. Female Wood Duck (pg. 143) is smaller and has white eye ring.

Stan's Notes: Familiar duck of lakes and ponds. Will return to place of birth. The name "Mallard" comes from the Latin *masculus*, meaning "male," referring to the habit of males not taking part in raising ducklings. Both male and female have white tails and white underwings. Black central tail feathers of male curl upward.

RING-NECKED PHEASANT
Phasianus colchicus

YEAR-ROUND

Size: 30-36" (76-90 cm), male, including tail
21-25" (53-63 cm), female, including tail

Male: Golden brown body with long tail. White ring around neck with purple, green, blue and red head.

Female: smaller, less flamboyant all-brown bird with long tail

Juvenile: similar to female, with shorter tail

Nest: ground; female builds; 1 brood per year

Eggs: 8-10; olive brown, unmarked

Incubation: 23-25 days; female incubates

Fledging: 11-12 days; female leads young to food

Migration: non-migrator

Food: insects, seeds, fruit, will come to ground feeders

Compare: At least twice the size of the Northern Bobwhite (pg. 115). Pheasant has a longer tail, and the male is brightly colored.

Stan's Notes: Introduced from China in the late 1800s. Now common throughout the U.S. Like many game birds, their numbers vary greatly, making them common some years and scarce others. The name "Ring-necked" refers to the thin white ring around the male's neck. The name "Pheasant" comes from the Greek word *phaisianos*, meaning "a bird of the River Phasis," which is now known as the River Rioni, located in Europe. Listen for the male's cackling call to attract females.

WILD TURKEY
Meleagris gallopavo

YEAR-ROUND

Size: 36-48" (90-120 cm)

Male: Large, plump brown and bronze bird with striking blue and red bare head. Fan tail and long, straight black beard in center of chest. Spurs on legs.

Female: thinner and less striking than male, usually lacking breast beard

Juvenile: same as adult

Nest: ground; female builds; 1 brood per year

Eggs: 10-12; buff white with dull brown markings

Incubation: 27-28 days; female incubates

Fledging: 6-10 days; female leads young to food

Migration: non-migrator

Food: insects, seeds, fruit

Compare: This bird is distinctive and unlikely to be confused with others.

Stan's Notes: Eliminated from Indiana by the turn of the twentieth century due to market hunting and loss of habitat, they were reintroduced in the 1950-60s. Males hold "harems" of up to 20 females. Strong fliers, they can approach 60 mph. Able to fly straight up, then away. Eyesight three times better than humans. Their hearing is also excellent; able to hear competing males up to one mile away. Nearly became our national bird, but lost by one vote to the Bald Eagle. They roost in trees at night. The bird from which the domestic turkey was bred. Largest game bird in Indiana. Males are called toms, females are hens and young are called poults.

RUBY-CROWNED KINGLET
Regulus calendula

Size: 4" (10 cm)

Male: Small, teardrop-shaped gray green bird with two white wing bars and a hidden ruby-colored crown. White eye ring.

Female: same as male, lacks ruby crown

Juvenile: same as adult

Nest: pendulous; female builds; 1 brood per year

Eggs: 4-5; white with brown markings

Incubation: 11-12 days; female incubates

Fledging: 11-12 days; female and male feed young

Migration: complete, to southern states, Mexico and Central America

Food: insects, berries

Compare: Similar to the Golden-crowned Kinglet (pg. 165), but crown is ruby colored.

Stan's Notes: Most commonly seen during spring and autumn migrations. It takes a quick eye to see the male's ruby crown. Look for small bird flitting around thick shrubs low to the ground. The name "Kinglet" comes from the Anglo-Saxon word *cyning*, or "king," referring to its ruby crown, and the diminutive suffix "let," meaning "small." The second smallest bird in Indiana. Builds an unusual pendulous (sac-like) nest, intricately woven and suspended from a branch overlapped by leaves. Usually the nest is hung high in mature trees. It is decorated on the outside with colored lichens and mosses stuck together with spider webs.

WINTER

GOLDEN-CROWNED KINGLET
Regulus satrapa

Size: 4" (10 cm)

Male: A tiny, plump gray green bird with a distinctive yellow and orange patch with black border on crown. White eyebrow mark. Two white wing bars.

Female: same as male, but has a yellow crown, lacking any orange

Juvenile: same as adult

Nest: pendulous; female builds; 1-2 broods a year

Eggs: 5-9; white or creamy with brown markings

Incubation: 14-15 days; female incubates

Fledging: 14-19 days; female and male feed young

Migration: complete to southern states, Mexico and Central America

Food: insects, fruit, tree sap

Compare: Similar to Ruby-crowned Kinglet (pg. 163), but Golden-crowned has an obvious crown. Smaller than the female American Goldfinch (pg. 249), which lacks any crown marking.

Stan's Notes: Common during winter in southern Indiana. Often seen in flocks that include chickadees, nuthatches, woodpeckers, Brown Creepers and Ruby-crowned Kinglets. Has a habit of flicking its wings when moving around. Unusual hanging nest is often made of moss, lichens and spider webs, and lined with bark and feathers. Can have so many eggs in its small nest that eggs are in two layers. Drinks tree sap and feeds by gleaning insects from trees. Can be very tame and approachable.

RED-BREASTED NUTHATCH
Sitta canadensis

Size: 4½" (11 cm)

Male: Small gray-backed bird with a black cap and prominent eye line. Rust red breast and belly.

Female: gray cap, pale undersides

Juvenile: same as female

Nest: cavity; female builds; 1 brood per year

Eggs: 5-6; white with red brown markings

Incubation: 11-12 days; female incubates

Fledging: 14-20 days; female and male feed young

Migration: irruptive, moves around the state to find food

Food: insects, seeds, will come to seed and suet feeders

Compare: Smaller than the White-breasted Nuthatch (pg. 177), has a red breast instead of white.

Stan's Notes: Common during some winters and scarce during others, Red-breasted Nuthatch behaves like the White-breasted Nuthatch, climbing down tree trunks head-first. Similar to chickadees, visits seed feeders, quickly grabbing one seed and flying off to crack it open. Will wedge a seed into a crevice and pound it open with several sharp blows. The name "Nuthatch" comes from the Middle English moniker *nuthak*, referring to the bird's habit of wedging a seed into a crevice and hacking it open. Look for them in mature conifers, frequently extracting seeds from cones. Doesn't excavate cavity as a chickadee might; rather, it takes over a former woodpecker or chickadee cavity.

YEAR-ROUND

BLACK-CAPPED CHICKADEE
Poecile atricapillus

Size: 5" (13 cm)

Male: Familiar gray bird with a black cap and throat patch. White chest and a tan belly. Small white wing marks.

Female: same as male

Juvenile: same as adult

Nest: cavity; female and male build or excavate; 1 brood per year

Eggs: 5-7; white, fine brown markings

Incubation: 11-13 days; female and male incubate

Fledging: 14-18 days; female and male feed young

Migration: non-migrator

Food: insects, seeds, fruit, attracted to seed and suet feeders

Compare: Identical to Carolina Chickadee (pg. 171), except in song. Carolina's song is a higher and faster version of the Black-capped Chickadee's. Tufted Titmouse (pg. 179) is larger than Black-capped Chickadee and has a crest.

Stan's Notes: A common backyard bird that can be attracted with a simple nest box. Makes nest mostly of green moss and lined with animal fur. Usually the first bird to find a new bird feeder. Can have different calls in various regions. Can be easily tamed and hand fed. Needs to feed every day during winter; consequently seen foraging for food during even the worst winter storms.

CAROLINA CHICKADEE
Poecile carolinensis

YEAR-ROUND

Size: 5" (13 cm)

Male: A mostly gray bird with a black cap and chin. White face and chest with a tan belly. Darker gray tail.

Female: same as male

Juvenile: same as adult

Nest: cavity; female and male build or excavate; 1-2 broods per year

Eggs: 5-7; white with reddish brown markings

Incubation: 11-12 days; female and male incubate

Fledging: 13-17 days; female and male feed young

Migration: non-migrator

Food: insects, seeds, fruit, comes to seed and suet feeders

Compare: Identical to the Black-capped Chickadee (pg. 169), except in song. Tufted Titmouse (pg. 179) has an erect crest, and lacks the black cap and chin.

Stan's Notes: A common bird of southern Indiana. It will breed (hybridize) with the more northern Black-capped Chickadee where they meet. Can be attracted with a nest box with a 1¼-inch entrance hole. Females will give a loud snake-like hiss when disturbed on the nest. Often seen with other birds (mixed flock) during winter. A friendly bird that can be tamed and hand fed. Difficult to tell apart from the Black-capped Chickadee; best distinction is the song. Carolina's song is higher, faster version of the familiar "chika-dee-dee-dee-dee."

male

female

YELLOW-RUMPED WARBLER
Dendroica coronata

Size: 5-6" (13-15 cm)

Male: Slate gray bird with black streaks on breast. Yellow patch on the head, flanks and rump. White chin and belly. Two white wing bars.

Female: similar to male, duller in color, mostly brown and white with matching yellow patches

Juvenile: similar to female

Nest: cup; female builds; 2 broods per year

Eggs: 4-5; white with brown markings

Incubation: 12-13 days; female incubates

Fledging: 10-12 days; female and male feed young

Migration: complete, to southern states, Mexico and Central America

Food: insects, berries, rarely comes to suet feeders

Compare: Similar to other warblers, look for combination of yellow patches on head, flank and rump. Magnolia Warbler (pg. 253) is more yellow than Yellow-rumped Warbler. Prairie Warbler (pg. 257) has olive back with chestnut-colored streaks. Common Yellowthroat (pg. 251) has yellow breast, compared with Yellow-rumped Warbler's spots of yellow.

Stan's Notes: One of the most common warblers, seen in flocks of hundreds during spring and fall migrations, and one of only a few warblers to spend the winter in southern Indiana. Formerly called the Myrtle Warbler. Sometimes called Butter-butts due to yellow patch on rump. Males molt to a dull color similar to females each winter, retaining yellow patches. Familiar call is a robust "chip."

female pg. 81

male

WINTER

DARK-EYED JUNCO
Junco hyemalis

Size: 5½" (14 cm)

Male: A round bird with a slate gray-to-charcoal chest, head and back. White belly, pink bill and dark eye. Since outermost tail feathers are white, tail appears as a white V in flight.

Female: same as male, only tan-to-brown color

Juvenile: similar to female, with streaked chest and head

Nest: cup; female and male build; 2 broods per year

Eggs: 3-5; white with reddish brown markings

Incubation: 12-13 days; female incubates

Fledging: 10-13 days; male and female feed young

Migration: complete, all across United States

Food: seeds, insects, will come to seed feeders

Compare: Rarely confused with other birds. Large flocks come to feed under bird feeders.

Stan's Notes: One of Indiana's most common winter birds. Usually seen on the ground in small flocks. Migrates from Canada to Indiana and beyond. Females tend to migrate farther south than males. Look for white outer tail feathers that flash in flight. Several species of juncos have now been combined into one, simply called Dark-eyed Junco. Most comfortable on the ground, juncos "double-scratch" with both feet to expose seeds and insects. Consume many weed seeds. A flocking bird, it adheres to a rigid social hierarchy with dominant birds chasing less dominant birds.

WHITE-BREASTED NUTHATCH
Sitta carolinensis

YEAR-ROUND

Size: 5-6" (13-15 cm)

Male: Slate gray with a white face and belly, and black cap and nape. Long thin bill, slightly upturned. Chestnut undertail.

Female: similar to male, gray cap and nape

Juvenile: same as adult

Nest: cavity; female and male build; 1 brood per year

Eggs: 5-7; white with brown markings

Incubation: 11-12 days; female incubates

Fledging: 13-14 days; female and male feed young

Migration: non-migrator

Food: insects, seeds, will come to seed and suet feeders

Compare: The Red-breasted Nuthatch (pg. 167) is smaller, and has rusty belly and distinctive black eye line.

Stan's Notes: The Nuthatch's habit of hopping head-first down tree trunks helps them see insects and eggs that birds climbing up the trunk might miss. The name "Nuthatch" comes from the Middle English moniker *nuthak*, referring to the bird's habit of wedging a seed into a crevice and hacking it open. Often seen in mixed flocks of chickadees, Brown Creepers and Downy Woodpeckers. Mated pairs remain together all year, defending their small territories. Listen for characteristic springtime call, "whi-whi-whi-whi," given during February and March. One of 17 worldwide nuthatch species. Incredible climbing agility comes from an extra long hind toe claw or nail, nearly twice the size of front toe claws.

YEAR-ROUND

TUFTED TITMOUSE
Baeolophus bicolor

Size: 6" (15 cm)

Male: Slate gray bird with a white chest and belly. Flanks washed in rusty brown. Gray legs and dark eyes. Pointed crest.

Female: same as male

Juvenile: same as adult

Nest: cavity, takes over former woodpecker hole; female builds; 2 broods per year

Eggs: 5-7; white with brown markings

Incubation: 13-14 days; female incubates

Fledging: 15-18 days; female and male feed young

Migration: non-migrator

Food: insects, seeds, fruit, comes to seed and suet feeders

Compare: Closely related to, but slightly larger than, the Black-capped Chickadee (pg. 169) and Carolina Chickadee (pg. 171). Chickadees lack crest of the Tufted Titmouse. Similar in size and color to the White-breasted Nuthatch (pg. 177), but Nuthatch doesn't have a crest.

Stan's Notes: Prefix "Tit" comes from a Scandinavian word meaning "little." Suffix "mouse" is derived from the Old English word *mase*, which means "bird." Simply translated, it is "a small bird." Notorious for pulling hair from sleeping dogs, cats and squirrels to line their nests. Attracted with nest boxes. Usually seen only one or two at a time. Male feeds female during courtship and nesting.

EASTERN PHOEBE
Sayornis phoebe

Size: 7" (18 cm)

Male: Gray green bird with dark wings, light olive green belly and a thin dark bill.

Female: same as male

Juvenile: same as adult

Nest: cup; female builds; 2 broods per year

Eggs: 4-5; white, unmarked

Incubation: 15-16 days; female incubates

Fledging: 15-16 days; male and female feed young

Migration: complete, to southern states and Mexico

Food: insects

Compare: Like most olive green birds, it is hard to distinguish any identifying markings. Eastern Phoebe lacks any white eye ring. Easier to identify by well-enunciated song, "fee-bee," or characteristic of hawking for insects.

Stan's Notes: A sparrow-sized bird often seen on the end of a dead branch. It sits waiting for a passing insect, flies out to catch it and then returns to the same branch, a process called hawking. Will build nest under the eaves of a house, under a bridge or in culverts. The nest, made of mud, grass and moss, is lined with hair and feathers. Name derived from its characteristic song, "fee-bee," repeated over and over from the tops of dead branches. Phoebe has a habit of pumping and spreading its tail when perched.

EASTERN KINGBIRD
Tyrannus tyrannus

Size: 8" (20 cm)

Male: Mostly black gray bird with white belly and chin. Black head and tail with a distinctive white band across the end of the tail. Has a concealed red crown that is rarely seen.

Female: same as male

Juvenile: same as adult

Nest: cup; male and female build; 1 brood per year

Eggs: 3-4; white with brown markings

Incubation: 16-18 days; female incubates

Fledging: 16-18 days; female and male feed young

Migration: complete, to Central and South Americas

Food: insects, fruit

Compare: Rarely confused with other birds. Medium-sized bird, smaller than American Robin (pg. 191). Look for the white band along the end of the tail to identify.

Stan's Notes: A common bird of open fields and prairies. Perceived as having an attitude, acting unafraid of other birds and chasing the larger ones. Bold behavior gave rise to its common name, King. Perches on tall branches, watching for insects. After flying out to catch them, returns to the same perch, a technique called hawking. Males and females return to mating grounds and will defend a territory together.

GREAT CRESTED FLYCATCHER
Myiarchus crinitus

SUMMER

Size:	8" (20 cm)
Male:	Gray head with a prominent crest. Gray back and throat with a bright yellow belly extending down under reddish brown tail. Lower bill is yellow at base.
Female:	same as male
Juvenile:	same as adult
Nest:	cavity; female and male build; 1 brood per year
Eggs:	4-6; white or buff with brown markings
Incubation:	13-15 days; female incubates
Fledging:	14-21 days; female and male feed young
Migration:	complete, to Mexico and Central America
Food:	insects, fruit
Compare:	The Eastern Kingbird (pg. 183) has a white band across the tail. Similar to the Eastern Phoebe (pg. 181), but Great Crested Flycatcher has obvious crest and yellow belly.

Stan's Notes: A common bird of just about any wooded area, it lives high up in the trees, rarely coming to the ground. Often heard before seen. Feeds by gleaning insects from the leaves of trees. Nests in old woodpecker holes, but can be attracted to a nest box placed high in a tree with an entrance hole of 1½ -2½ inches. Often stuffs nest with a collection of fur, feathers, string and snakeskins. Breeds throughout Indiana.

SUMMER

GRAY CATBIRD
Dumetella carolinensis

Size: 9" (22.5 cm)

Male: A handsome slate gray bird with a black crown. Long, thin black bill. Often seen with tail lifted, exposing chestnut-colored patch under tail.

Female: same as male

Juvenile: same as adult

Nest: cup; female and male build; 2 broods per year

Eggs: 4-6; blue green, unmarked

Incubation: 12-13 days; female incubates

Fledging: 10-11 days; female and male feed young

Migration: complete, to southern states

Food: insects, fruit

Compare: Larger than Eastern Phoebe (pg. 181), it lacks the Phoebe's olive belly. Similar size to Eastern Kingbird (pg. 183), but it lacks the Kingbird's white belly and white tail band.

Stan's Notes: A secretive bird that the Chippewa Indians named Bird That Cries With Grief due to its raspy call. Its call sounds like a house cat's mewing, hence its common name. Often mimics other birds, rarely repeating the same phrases. Will only nest in thick shrubs and is more often heard than seen. Quickly flies back into the shrubs when approached. If a cowbird introduces an egg into a catbird nest, the catbird will quickly break it, then eject it.

red morph

gray morph

YEAR-ROUND

EASTERN SCREECH-OWL
Megascops asio

Size: 9" (22.5 cm)

Male: Small "eared" owl that occurs in one of two permanent color morphs. Is either mottled with gray and white, or is red brown (rust) with white. Bright yellow eyes.

Female: same as male

Juvenile: lighter gray than adult, may lack the ear tufts

Nest: cavity; former woodpecker cavity; 1 brood per year

Eggs: 4-5; white, unmarked

Incubation: 25-26 days; female incubates, male feeds female during incubation

Fledging: 26-27 days; male and female feed young

Migration: non-migrator

Food: large insects, small mammals, birds, snakes

Compare: The only small owl in the state with ear tufts. Can be gray or rust-colored.

Stan's Notes: A common owl active at dusk and during the night. Excellent hearing and eyesight. Seldom gives a screeching call; more commonly gives a tremulous, descending whiny trill that sounds like it came from the sound track of a scary movie. Will nest in wooden nest box. Often seen sunning themselves at nest box holes during winter. Male and female may roost together at night, and are thought to mate for life. Different colorations are known as morphs. The gray morph is more common than the red.

male

female

AMERICAN ROBIN
Turdus migratorius

YEAR-ROUND

Size: 9-11" (22.5-28 cm)

Male: Familiar gray bird with rusty red chest, nearly black head and tail, and black streaks on white chin. White eye ring.

Female: similar to male, but has a gray head and duller chest

Juvenile: similar to female, but has speckled chest and brown back

Nest: cup; female builds with help from male; 2 broods per year

Eggs: 4-7; pale blue, unmarked

Incubation: 12-14 days; female incubates

Fledging: 14-16 days; female and male feed young

Migration: complete, to southern states and Central America, small percentage will not migrate

Food: insects, fruit, berries, worms

Compare: Familiar bird to all.

Stan's Notes: Most people don't realize how easy it is to tell the difference between the male and female robin. Look for the male's dark, nearly black head, compared with the female's gray head. Robins are not listening for worms when they cock their heads to one side or the other. They are looking with eyes that are placed far back on the sides of their heads. Small percentage will not migrate, but spend the winter in low swampy areas where they search for leftover berries and insect eggs.

displaying

NORTHERN MOCKINGBIRD
Mimus polyglottos

YEAR-ROUND

Size: 10" (25 cm)

Male: Silvery gray head and back with light gray chest and belly. White wing patches, seen in flight or during display. Tail mostly black with white outer tail feathers. Black bill.

Female: same as male

Juvenile: overall dull gray with a heavily streaked chest, gray bill

Nest: cup; female and male build; 2 broods per year, sometimes more

Eggs: 3-5; blue green with brown markings

Incubation: 12-13 days; female incubates

Fledging: 11-13 days; female and male feed young

Migration: partial migrator in northern states

Food: insects, fruit

Compare: Similar to the Brown Thrasher (pg. 119), but Thrasher is rusty red with a streaked chest. Gray Catbird (pg. 187) is slate gray and lacks Mockingbird's white wing patches. Look for Mockingbird to spread its wings, flash its white wing patches and wag its tail from side to side.

Stan's Notes: Very animated, both male and female perform elaborate mating dances by facing each other, heads and tails erect. They run towards each other, flashing white wing patches, then retreat to nearby cover. Known to imitate other birds, called vocal mimicry, hence its common name. Young males often sing at night.

193

soaring

juvenile

SHARP-SHINNED HAWK
Accipiter striatus

YEAR-ROUND

Size: 10-14" (25-36 cm)

Male: A small woodland hawk with gray brown back and head. Rusty red breast. Long tail with several dark tail bands, widest band at end of squared-off tail. Red eye.

Female: same as male, only larger

Juvenile: same size as adult, with brown back and heavily streaked breast, yellow eye

Nest: platform; female builds; 1 brood per year

Eggs: 4-5; white with brown markings

Incubation: 32-35 days; female incubates

Fledging: 24-27 days; female and male feed young

Migration: complete, southern states, Mexico and Central America

Food: birds, small mammals

Compare: Nearly identical to Cooper's Hawk (pg. 199), only smaller. Look for squared end of tail on Sharp-shinned, compared with round end of Cooper's.

Stan's Notes: A common hawk of backyards and woodland, they are often seen swooping in on birds visiting feeders. Short rounded wings and long tail allow this hawk to navigate through thick stands of trees in pursuit of prey. Common name comes from the sharp keel on the leading edge of its "shin," although it is actually below rather than above the bird's ankle on the tarsus bone of foot. The tarsus in most birds is round. In flight, head doesn't protrude as far as the head of the Cooper's Hawk.

ROCK PIGEON
Columba livia

YEAR-ROUND

Size: 13" (33 cm)

Male: No set color pattern. Gray to white with patches of iridescent greens and blues, usually with a light rump patch.

Female: same as male

Juvenile: same as adult

Nest: platform; female builds; 3-4 broods per year

Eggs: 1-2; white, unmarked

Incubation: 18-20 days; female and male incubate

Fledging: 25-26 days; female and male feed young

Migration: non-migrator

Food: seeds

Compare: Larger than light-brown-colored Mourning Dove (pg. 127).

Stan's Notes: Also known as Domestic Pigeon, it was introduced to North America from Europe by early settlers. Most common around cities and barnyards, where it scratches for seeds. The wide color variation comes from years of selective breeding while in captivity. Parents feed young a regurgitated liquid called crop-milk the first few days of life. One of the few birds that can drink without tilting its head back. Nests under bridges, on buildings, balconies, barns and sheds. Once poisoned as a "nuisance city bird," many cities have Peregrine Falcons that feed on Rock Pigeons, keeping their numbers in check.

soaring

juvenile

YEAR-ROUND

COOPER'S HAWK
Accipiter cooperii

Size: 14-20" (36-50 cm)

Male: A medium hawk with short wings and a long rounded tail with several black bands. Rusty chest and dark wing tips. Slate gray back. Bright yellow spot at base of gray bill, called a cere. Red eye.

Female: similar to male, only slightly larger

Juvenile: brown back with brown streaks on chest, yellow eye

Nest: platform; male and female build; 1 brood per year

Eggs: 2-4; greenish with brown markings

Incubation: 32-36 days; female and male incubate

Fledging: 28-32 days; male and female feed young

Migration: non-migrator to partial migrator, to southern states and Mexico

Food: small birds, mammals

Compare: Nearly identical to the Sharp-shinned Hawk (pg. 195), only larger, darker gray and with a rounded-off tail.

Stan's Notes: A common hawk of the woodland. In flight, look for its large head, short wings and proportionately long tail. Short stubby wings help it maneuver between trees while pursuing small birds. Will come to feeders, hunting for unaware birds. Flies with long glides followed by a few quick flaps. Known to ambush their prey, they will fly into heavy brush or even run on the ground in pursuit. Nestlings have gray eyes that become bright yellow at one year and later, dark red.

male

female pg. 155

NORTHERN HARRIER
Circus cyaneus

YEAR-ROUND

Size: 24" (60 cm)

Male: A slim, low-flying hawk. Silver gray with large white rump patch and white belly. Faint narrow bands across the tail. Tips of wings black.

Female: dark brown back with brown-streaked breast and belly, large white rump patch, narrow black bands across tail, tips of wings black

Juvenile: similar to female, with orange breast

Nest: platform; female and male build; 1 brood per year

Eggs: 4-8; bluish white, unmarked

Incubation: 31-32 days; female incubates

Fledging: 30-35 days; male and female feed young

Migration: complete, southern states, Central America

Food: mice, snakes

Compare: Slimmer than Red-tailed Hawk (pg. 151). Look for black bands on tail and a white rump patch.

Stan's Notes: One of the easiest hawks to identify. Harriers glide just above ground, following the contours of the land while searching for prey. Wings are held just above the horizontal position, tilting back and forth in the wind, similar to Turkey Vultures. Formerly called Marsh Hawk due to its habit of hunting over marshes. Nests on the ground. At all ages, the Northern Harrier has distinctive owl-like face disks.

CANADA GOOSE
Branta canadensis

YEAR-ROUND

Size: 25-43" (63-109 cm)

Male: Large gray goose with black neck and head, with a white chin or cheek strap.

Female: same as male

Juvenile: same as adult

Nest: ground; female builds; 1 brood per year

Eggs: 5-10; white, unmarked

Incubation: 25-30 days; female incubates

Fledging: 42-55 days; male and female teach young to feed

Migration: non-migrator to partial migrator, to southern states

Food: aquatic plants, insects, seeds

Compare: A very common bird, hardly ever confused with any other bird.

Stan's Notes: Once not very common, they have adapted to our changed environment very well. Adults will mate for many years, and will only start to breed in their third year. Males often act as sentinels, standing on the edge of the group and bobbing their heads up and down, becoming very aggressive to anyone who approaches. Will hiss as if to display displeasure. Adults molt primary flight feathers while raising young, rendering family groups flightless at the same time. Several subspecies vary geographically around the U.S. Generally they are paler in color in eastern groups, and darker in the western. Their size decreases northward, with the smallest subspecies found on the Arctic tundra. Introduced into several parts of the state, they are now breeding in Indiana and are common year-round residents.

MIGRATION
SUMMER

SANDHILL CRANE
Grus canadensis

Size: 40-48" (102-120 cm); up to 7-foot wingspan

Male: Elegant gray bird with long legs and neck. Wings and body often stained rusty brown. Scarlet red cap. Red eye.

Female: same as male

Juvenile: dull brown without red cap, yellow eye

Nest: platform, on the ground; female and male build; 1 brood per year

Eggs: 2; olive with brown markings

Incubation: 28-32 days; female and male incubate

Fledging: 65 days; female and male feed young

Migration: complete, to southern states and Mexico

Food: insects, fruit, worms, plants, amphibians

Compare: Similar size as Great Blue Heron (pg. 207), but the Sandhill has a shorter bill and a red patch on head. The Great Blue Heron flies with its neck held in an S shape, unlike the Sandhill's straight neck.

Stan's Notes: Usually seen in large undisturbed fields near water. Often heard before seen, they have a very distinctive rattling call. Plumage often appears rust brown because of staining from mud during preening. Characteristic flight with upstroke quicker than down. For their spectacular mating dance the performers face each other, bow and jump into the air while uttering a loud cackling sound and flapping wings. Often flips sticks and grass into the air during dance.

GREAT BLUE HERON
Ardea herodias

Size: 42-52" (107-132 cm)

Male: Tall gray heron with black eyebrow extending into several long plumes off back of head. Long yellow bill. Feathers at base of neck drop down in a kind of necklace.

Female: same as male

Juvenile: same as adult, but more brown than gray, with a black crown and no plumes

Nest: platform; male and female build; 1 brood per year

Eggs: 3-5; blue green, unmarked

Incubation: 27-28 days; female and male incubate

Fledging: 56-60 days; male and female feed young

Migration: complete, to southern states, Central and South Americas

Food: small fish, frogs, insects, snakes

Compare: Similar size as the Sandhill Crane (pg. 205), but lacks the Sandhill's red crown. Sandhill flies with neck held straight, unlike Great Blue Heron's S-shaped neck.

YEAR-ROUND
SUMMER

Stan's Notes: One of the most common herons, it often barks like a dog when startled. Seen stalking small fish in shallow water. Will strike at mice, squirrels and just about anything else it might come across. Flies holding neck in an S shape, with its long legs trailing straight out behind. Wings are held in cupped fashion during flight. Nests in colonies of up to 100 birds. Nests in treetops near or over open water.

male

female

RUBY-THROATED HUMMINGBIRD
Archilochus colubris

Size: 3-3½" (7.5-9 cm)

Male: Tiny iridescent green bird with black throat patch that reflects bright ruby red in sunlight.

Female: same as male, lacking throat patch

Juvenile: same as female

Nest: cup; female builds; 1-2 broods per year

Eggs: 2; white, unmarked

Incubation: 12-14 days; female incubates

Fledging: 14-18 days; female feeds young

Migration: complete, to southern states, Mexico and Central America

Food: nectar, insects

Compare: No other bird this small. Sphinx Moth hovers at flowers like Hummingbird, but has clear wings and a mouth part that looks like a straw, which coils up when not at flower. Moves much slower than Hummingbird and can be approached.

Stan's Notes: Wings create a humming noise, flapping 50 to 60 times per second or faster during chasing flights. Able to hover, fly up and down, and is the only bird to fly backwards. Constructs nest with plant material and spider webs, gluing pieces of lichen on outside of nest for camouflage. Attracted to tubular red flowers. Weighing only two to three grams, it takes about five average-sized hummingbirds to equal the weight of a single chickadee. Heart beats at an incredible 1,260 times a minute and breathes 250 times a minute. Does not sing, but will chatter or buzz to communicate.

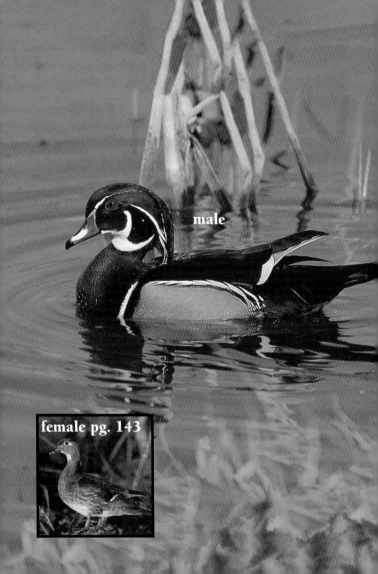

male

female pg. 143

WOOD DUCK
Aix sponsa

YEAR-ROUND
SUMMER

Size: 17-20" (43-50 cm)

Male: A small, highly ornamented dabbling duck with a green head and crest, red eye, and patterned with white and black. Rusty chest and white belly.

Female: brown, similar size and shape to male, has bright white eye ring and not so obvious crest, blue patch on wing often hidden

Juvenile: same as female

Nest: cavity; female lines former woodpecker cavity; 1 brood per year

Eggs: 10-15; creamy white, unmarked

Incubation: 28-36 days; female incubates

Fledging: 56-68 days; female teaches young to feed

Migration: complete, to southern states

Food: aquatic insects, plants, seeds

Compare: Smaller than the male Northern Shoveler (pg. 215). Lacks Shoveler's long wide bill.

Stan's Notes: A common duck of quiet, shallow backwater ponds. Nearly extinct around 1900 due to over-hunting, but doing well now. Nests in old woodpecker holes or nest boxes. Often seen flying deep within a forest or perched high up on branches of trees. Female enters nest cavity from full flight. Females will lay eggs in neighboring female nest, called egg dumping, resulting in some clutches in excess of 20 eggs. Young remain in nest cavity only 24 hours after hatching, then jump from up to 30 feet to the ground or water to follow their mother. After that, they never return to the nest.

GREEN HERON
Butorides virescens

SUMMER

Size: 16-22" (40-56 cm)

Male: A short stocky heron with a blue-green back, and rusty red neck and chest. Dark green crest. Short legs, normally yellow, but turn bright orange during breeding season.

Female: same as male

Juvenile: similar to adult, with blue-gray back and white-streaked chest and neck

Nest: platform; female and male build; 2 broods per year

Eggs: 2-4; light green, unmarked

Incubation: 21-25 days; female and male incubate

Fledging: 35-36 days; female and male feed young

Migration: complete, to South America

Food: fish, insects, aquatic plants

Compare: Much smaller than the Great Blue Heron (pg. 207). Look for a small heron stalking along lakeshore with dark green back.

Stan's Notes: Often gives an explosive rasping "skyew" when startled. Sometimes it looks like it doesn't have a neck, because it holds its head close to its body. Hunts for fish and aquatic insects by waiting along a shore or wades stealthily. Has been known to place an object like an insect on the water surface to attract fish to catch. Has a crest that it raises when excited.

male

female pg. 147

MIGRATION
WINTER

NORTHERN SHOVELER
Anas clypeata

Size: 20" (50 cm)

Male: A medium-sized duck with an iridescent green head, rusty sides and a white breast. Has an extraordinarily large spoon-shaped bill, almost always held pointed towards the water.

Female: same spoon-shaped bill, with brown and black all over and green speculum

Juvenile: same as female

Nest: ground; female builds; 1 brood per year

Eggs: 9-12; olive, unmarked

Incubation: 22-25 days; female incubates

Fledging: 30-60 days; female leads young to food

Migration: complete, to southern states and Central America

Food: aquatic insects, plants

Compare: Similar to the male Mallard (pg. 219), but Shoveler has a large, characteristic spoon-shaped bill. Larger than the average male Wood Duck (pg. 211) and lacks the Wood Duck's crest.

Stan's Notes: Seen in small flocks of five to ten, swimming low in water with large bills always pointed towards water, as if they're too heavy to lift. More commonly seen during spring migration. Feeds primarily by filtering tiny plants and insects from the water's surface with bill.

female pg. 235

male

COMMON MERGANSER
Mergus merganser

MIGRATION
WINTER

Size: 27" (69 cm)

Male: A long, thin, duck-like bird with a green head and black back. White sides, chest and neck. Long pointed bill.

Female: same size and shape as male, but with a rust red head, ragged "hair" on crest, gray body, white chest and long pointed bill

Juvenile: same as female

Nest: cavity; female lines former woodpecker cavity; 1 brood per year

Eggs: 9-11; ivory without markings

Incubation: 28-33 days; female incubates

Fledging: 70-80 days; female feeds young

Migration: complete, to southern states, Central America and Mexico

Food: fish, aquatic insects

Compare: Male Hooded Merganser (pg. 37) has white patch on head and rusty brown sides.

Stan's Notes: Mergansers are shallow water divers that feed on small fish in no more than 10 or 15 feet of water. More commonly seen along rivers than lakes. Their bills have a fine serrated-like edge to help catch slippery fish. Females often lay eggs in other merganser nests, called egg dumping, resulting in broods of up to 15 young per mother. The male leaves the female as soon as she starts to incubate eggs. Young that lose their mothers will be accepted by other merganser mothers with young.

female pg. 157

male

MALLARD
Anas platyrhynchos

YEAR-ROUND

Size: 27-28" (69-71 cm)

Male: Large, bulbous green head, white necklace and rust brown or chestnut-colored chest. Combination of gray and white on sides. Yellow bill, legs and feet.

Female: all-brown duck with orange and black bill and small blue and white wing mark, called a speculum

Juvenile: same as female, but with yellow bill

Nest: ground; female builds; 1 brood per year

Eggs: 7-10; greenish to whitish, unmarked

Incubation: 26-30 days; female incubates

Fledging: 42-52 days; female leads young to food

Migration: complete, to southern states, small percentage non-migrator

Food: seeds, plants, aquatic insects, ground feeders offering corn

Compare: The male Northern Shoveler (pg. 215) has a white chest with rust on sides and dark spoon-shaped bill.

Stan's Notes: Familiar duck of lakes and ponds. Will return to place of birth. The name "Mallard" comes from the Latin *masculus*, meaning "male," referring to the habit of males not taking part in raising ducklings. Both male and female have white tails and white underwings. Black central tail feathers of male curl upward.

male

female pg. 247

AMERICAN REDSTART
Setophaga ruticilla

SUMMER

Size: 5" (13 cm)

Male: A small, striking black bird with contrasting patches of orange on sides, wings and tail. White belly.

Female: olive brown with yellow patches instead of the male's orange, white belly

Juvenile: same as female, immature males tinged orange for first year

Nest: cup; female builds; 1 brood per year

Eggs: 3-5; off-white with brown markings

Incubation: 12 days; female incubates

Fledging: 9 days; female and male feed young

Migration: complete, to Mexico, Central and South Americas

Food: insects, seeds, berries rarely

Compare: The male Red-winged Blackbird (pg. 9) and the male Baltimore Oriole (pg. 223) are considerably larger, at roughly eight inches. Only small black and orange bird flitting around tops of trees.

Stan's Notes: A common and widespread warbler in Indiana. Prefers large unbroken tracts of forest. Appears to be hyperactive when feeding, hovering, and darting back and forth to glean insects from leaves. Look for flashing black and orange color high in the trees. They often droop wings and fan tails just before launching out to catch an insect.

male

female pg. 261

BALTIMORE ORIOLE
Icterus galbula

SUMMER

Size: 7-8" (18-20 cm)

Male: Bright, flaming orange bird with black head and black extending down nape of neck onto the back. Black wings with white and orange wing bars. Orange tail with black streaks. Gray bill and dark eye.

Female: pale yellow bird with gray brown wings, white wing bars, gray bill and dark eye

Juvenile: same as female

Nest: pendulous; female builds; 1 brood per year

Eggs: 4-5; bluish with brown markings

Incubation: 12-14 days; female incubates

Fledging: 12-14 days; female and male feed young

Migration: complete, to Mexico, Central and South Americas

Food: insects, fruit, nectar, will come to orange halves and nectar feeders

Compare: The male Orchard Oriole (pg. 225) is much darker orange than the Baltimore's flaming orange. Male American Redstart (pg. 221) is smaller and has more black than orange.

Stan's Notes: Fantastic songsters, these birds are often heard before seen. Easily attracted to a feeder offering grape jelly, orange halves or sugar water (nectar). Parents bring young to feeders. They build their sock-like nest at the outermost branches of tall trees. They often return to the same area year after year. Some of the last birds to arrive in spring (May) and first to leave in fall (September). They sit in the tops of the trees feeding on caterpillars.

female pg. 263

male

ORCHARD ORIOLE
Icterus spurius

SUMMER

Size: 7-8" (18-20 cm)

Male: Dull orange bird with black head and black extending down the back. Black chin, wings and tail. A single white wing bar. Long, thin black bill with a small gray mark on lower mandible (jaw).

Female: olive green back with a dull yellow belly, two white wing bars on dark gray wings

Juvenile: similar as female

Nest: pendulous; female builds; 1 brood per year

Eggs: 3-5; pale blue to white with brown markings

Incubation: 11-12 days; female and male incubate

Fledging: 11-14 days; female and male feed young

Migration: complete, to Central Mexico and northern South America

Food: insects, fruit, comes to fruit/nectar feeders

Compare: Similar to male Baltimore Oriole (pg. 223), but the male Orchard Oriole has a much darker orange body.

Stan's Notes: Prefers open woods and orchards, hence its common name. They eat insects until wild fruits start to ripen. One of the last birds to arrive in spring and one of the first to leave each fall, spending only about three to four months in Indiana. More common in southern Indiana. Usually nests alone, but sometimes in small colonies. Parents bring young to jelly and orange half feeders shortly after fledging. Many people mistakenly think the orioles have left during summer, but in fact, the birds are concentrating on finding insects to feed their young.

225

female pg. 71

male

HOUSE FINCH
Carpodacus mexicanus

YEAR-ROUND

Size: 5" (13 cm)

Male: Orange red face, chest and rump, with a dark marking behind eye. Brown wings streaked with white. A white belly with brown streaks. Brown cap.

Female: brown with heavily streaked white chest

Juvenile: similar to female

Nest: cup, sometimes in cavities; female builds; 2 broods per year

Eggs: 4-5; pale blue, lightly marked

Incubation: 12-14 days; female incubates

Fledging: 15-19 days; female and male feed young

Migration: non-migrator to partial migrator, moves around to find food

Food: seeds, fruit, leaf buds, will come to seed feeders

Compare: Very similar to male Purple Finch (pg. 229), lacking the Purple Finch's red cap. Look for the streaked chest and belly, and brown cap of male House Finch.

Stan's Notes: A relatively new bird to Indiana (first reported in 1976), it was originally introduced to Long Island, New York, in the 1940s from western America. A very social bird, it visits feeders in small flocks. Seems to prefer nesting in hanging flower baskets. Incubating female is fed by male. Loud and cheerful warbling song.

female pg. 85

male

PURPLE FINCH
Carpodacus purpureus

WINTER

Size: 6" (15 cm)

Male: Raspberry red head, cap, breast, back and rump. Brownish wings and tail.

Female: heavily streaked brown and white with a large white eye line

Juvenile: same as female

Nest: cup; female and male build; 1 brood per year

Eggs: 4-5; greenish blue with brown markings

Incubation: 12-13 days; female incubates

Fledging: 13-14 days; female and male feed young

Migration: irruptive, moves around the state to find food

Food: seeds, insects, fruit, will come to seed feeders

Compare: Redder than the orange red male House Finch (pg. 227), with a clear (no streaking) red breast. The male House Finch has a brown cap, compared with the male Purple Finch's red cap.

Stan's Notes: Usually only seen during winter, when flocks of Purple Finches leave their northern homes and move around looking for food. Travels in flocks of up to 50. Comes to seed feeders along with House Finches, making it hard to tell them apart. A rich loud song and a distinctive "tic" note is made only in flight. Not a purple color, the Latin name *purpureus* means "crimson" or other reddish color.

female
pg. 259

male

SUMMER

SCARLET TANAGER
Piranga olivacea

Size: 7" (18 cm)

Male: Bright scarlet red bird with jet black wings and tail. Ivory bill and dark eye.

Female: drab greenish yellow with olive wings and tail, whitish wing linings, dark eye

Juvenile: same as female

Nest: cup; female builds; 1 brood per year

Eggs: 4-5; blue green with brown markings

Incubation: 13-14 days; female incubates

Fledging: 9-11 days; female and male feed young

Migration: complete, to Central and South Americas

Food: insects, fruit

Compare: The male Northern Cardinal (pg. 233) has black mask and red bill, and lacks the black wings of the male Scarlet Tanager.

Stan's Notes: Male sheds (molts) its bright red plumage in the fall, appearing more like the female. Prefers mature unbroken woodland, where it hunts for insects high in the tops of trees. Requires a minimum of four acres for nesting; prefers eight acres. Tropical-looking birds, they arrive late in spring and leave early in autumn. Scarlet Tanager is included in some 240 tanager species in the world. Nearly all are brightly colored and live in the tropics. The name "Tanager" comes from a South American Tupi Indian word meaning "any small, brightly colored bird."

female pg. 109

male

juvenile

YEAR-ROUND

NORTHERN CARDINAL
Cardinalis cardinalis

Size: 8-9" (20-22.5 cm)

Male: All-red bird with a black mask extending from face down to chin and throat. Large red bill and crest.

Female: buff brown with tinges of red on crest and wings, same black mask and red bill

Juvenile: same as female, with blackish gray bill

Nest: cup; female builds; 2-3 broods per year

Eggs: 3-4; bluish white with brown markings

Incubation: 12-13 days; female and male incubate

Fledging: 9-10 days; female and male feed young

Migration: non-migrator

Food: seeds, insects, fruit, will come to seed feeders

Compare: The male Scarlet Tanager (pg. 231) has black wings and tail.

Stan's Notes: A familiar backyard bird, look for male feeding female during courtship. Male feeds young of first brood by himself while female builds second nest. Their name comes from the Latin word *cardinalis*, which means "important." Very territorial during spring, it will fight its own reflection in a window. Non-territorial in winter, they gather in small flocks of up to 20 birds. Both male and female sing, and can be heard anytime of year. Listen for their "whata-cheer-cheer-cheer" territorial call in spring.

male pg. 217

female

COMMON MERGANSER
Mergus merganser

Size: 27" (69 cm)

Female: A long, thin, duck-like bird with a rust red head and ragged "hair" on back of head. Gray body. White chest. Long pointed bill.

Male: same size and shape as female, but with a green head, black back, white sides, chest and neck, and long pointed bill

Juvenile: same as female

Nest: cavity; female lines former woodpecker cavity; 1 brood per year

Eggs: 9-11; ivory without markings

Incubation: 28-33 days; female incubates

Fledging: 70-80 days; female feeds young

Migration: complete, to southern states, Central America and Mexico

Food: fish, aquatic insects

Compare: The female Hooded Merganser (pg. 141) has a similar shape, but is much smaller with a brownish red head.

Stan's Notes: Mergansers are shallow water divers that feed on small fish in no more than 10 or 15 feet of water. More commonly seen along rivers than lakes. Their bills have a fine serrated-like edge to help catch slippery fish. Females often lay eggs in other merganser nests, called egg dumping, resulting in broods of up to 15 young per mother. The male leaves the female as soon as she starts to incubate eggs. Young that lose their mothers will be accepted by other merganser mothers with young.

235

winter

juvenile

breeding

RING-BILLED GULL
Larus delawarensis

YEAR-ROUND
MIGRATION
WINTER

Size: 19" (48 cm)

Male: A white bird with gray wings, black wing tips spotted with white, and white tail, as seen in flight. Yellow bill with a black ring near tip. Yellowish legs and feet. Winter or non-breeding adult has a speckled brown back of head and nape of neck.

Female: same as male

Juvenile: mostly gray version of winter adult, with a dark band at end of tail

Nest: ground; female and male build; 1 brood per year

Eggs: 2-4; off-white with brown markings

Incubation: 20-21 days; female and male incubate

Fledging: 20-40 days; female and male feed young

Migration: complete, to southern states and Mexico

Food: insects, fish, scavenges

Compare: Similar to Herring Gull (pg. 239), which has an orange mark on tip of lower bill. Herring Gull has pink legs and feet, and lacks Ring-billed Gull's black ring.

Stan's Notes: This is the common gull of garbage dumps and parking lots. They are expanding their range and remain farther north longer due to successful scavenging in cities. They acquire a new and different plumage in each of the first three autumns and don't attain adult plumage until third year. They attain ring on bill after first winter.

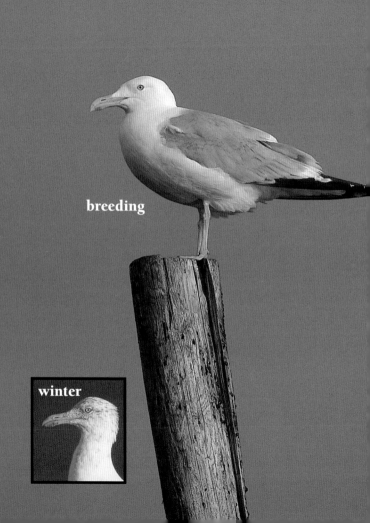

breeding

winter

HERRING GULL
Larus argentatus

Size: 23-26" (58-66 cm)

Male: Snow-white bird with slate gray wings and black wing tips with tiny white spots. Bill is yellow with an orange-red spot near tip of the lower bill. Pinkish legs. Winter plumage head and neck are dirty gray to brown.

Female: same as male

Juvenile: uniformly mottled brown to gray, black bill

Nest: ground; female and male build; 1 brood per year

Eggs: 2-3; olive with brown markings

Incubation: 24-28 days; female and male incubate

Fledging: 35-36 days; female and male feed young

Migration: complete, to coasts that remain unfrozen in North America

Food: fish, insects, clams, eggs, baby birds

Compare: Larger than the Ring-billed Gull (pg. 237), which has yellowish legs and a black ring around its bill, and lacks an orange-red dot on the lower mandible.

YEAR-ROUND
MIGRATION

Stan's Notes: An opportunistic bird, scavenging for food from dumpsters, but will also take other birds' eggs and young right from nest. Often drops clams and other shellfish from heights to break shells and get to the soft interior. Nests in colonies, returning to same site year after year. Lines nest with grasses and seaweed. Adults molt to a dirty gray in winter, looking similar to juveniles. Takes about four years for juveniles to obtain adult plumage.

blue morph

white morph

MIGRATION

SNOW GOOSE
Chen caerulescens

Size: 25-38" (63-96 cm)

Male: A mostly white goose with varying patches of black and brown. Black wing tips and pink bill and legs.

Female: same as male

Juvenile: overall dull gray with dark bill

Nest: ground; female builds; 1 brood per year

Eggs: 3-5; white, unmarked

Incubation: 23-25 days; female incubates

Fledging: 45-49 days; female and male teach young to feed

Migration: complete, to East coast, southern states and Mexico

Food: aquatic insects and plants

Compare: The Mute Swan (pg. 245) is nearly twice the average size of Snow Goose and lacks the black wing tips of Snow Goose. Smaller than the Canada Goose (pg. 203), lacking black neck and white chin strap.

Stan's Notes: Has a thick serrated bill to pull up plants. There are two color types, called phases or morphs. The gray phase is often called blue, with a white head, pink bill and legs, and gray chest and back. The other is pure white with black wing tips. Breeds in large colonies on the tundra of northern Canada. Females don't breed until two to three years old. Older females produce more eggs and are more successful than younger females. Seen by the thousands during migration.

in flight

GREAT EGRET
Ardea alba

MIGRATION
SUMMER

Size: 38" (96 cm)

Male: Tall, thin, elegant all-white bird with long, pointed yellow bill. Black stilt-like legs. Black feet.

Female: same as male

Juvenile: same as adult

Nest: platform; male and female build; 1 brood per year

Eggs: 2-3; light blue, unmarked

Incubation: 23-26 days; female and male incubate

Fledging: 43-49 days; female and male feed young

Migration: complete, to southern states, Mexico and Central America

Food: fish, aquatic insects, frogs, crayfish

Compare: Smaller in size and similar in shape to Great Blue Heron (pg. 207).

Stan's Notes: A tall and stately bird, the Great Egret slowly stalks shallow wetlands looking for small fish to spear with its long sharp bill. Nests in colonies of up to 100 birds. Now protected, they were hunted to near extinction for their long white plumage. The name "Egret" came from the French word *aigrette*, which means "ornamental tufts of plumes." The plumes are grown near the tail during breeding season.

YEAR-ROUND

MUTE SWAN
Cygnus olor

Size: 60" (152 cm)

Male: All white with prominent black knob at base of a large orange bill. Holds neck in an S shape with bill pointed towards the surface of the water.

Female: same as male

Juvenile: brown to gray, gray bill with black base lacks the prominent knob

Nest: ground; female and male build; 1 brood per year

Eggs: 4-8; light gray, lacking any markings

Incubation: 35-40 days; female incubates with help from male

Fledging: 115-150 days; female and male feed young

Migration: partial migrator, moves to areas with open water during winter

Food: aquatic insects and plants

Compare: Twice the average size of the Snow Goose (pg. 241) and lacks the Snow Goose's black wing tips.

Stan's Notes: An introduced species usually found in parks, zoos and golf courses is now found in the wild. Often swims with wings held arched over its back. Its neck is always held in an S shape. Can be an aggressive bird, giving a loud hiss when disturbed or threatened.

male pg. 221

female

AMERICAN REDSTART
Setophaga ruticilla

Size: 5" (13 cm)

Female: Olive brown with yellow patches on sides, wings and tail. White belly.

Male: small, striking black bird with contrasting patches of orange on sides, wings and tail, white belly

Juvenile: same as female, immature males tinged orange for first year

Nest: cup; female builds; 1 brood per year

Eggs: 3-5; off-white with brown markings

Incubation: 12 days; female incubates

Fledging: 9 days; female and male feed young

Migration: complete, to Mexico, Central and South Americas

Food: insects, seeds, berries rarely

Compare: Similar to female Yellow-rumped Warbler (pg. 173), but lacking the Warbler's yellow patch on rump.

Stan's Notes: A common and widespread warbler in Indiana. Prefers large unbroken tracts of forest. Appears to be hyperactive when feeding, hovering, and darting back and forth to glean insects from leaves. Look for flashing black and orange color high in the trees. They often droop wings and fan tails just before launching out to catch an insect.

male

winter male

female

AMERICAN GOLDFINCH
Carduelis tristis

YEAR-ROUND

Size: 5" (13 cm)

Male: A perky yellow bird with a black patch on forehead. Black tail with conspicuous white rump. Black wings with white wing bars. No marking on the chest. Dramatic change in color during winter, similar to female.

Female: dull olive yellow without a black forehead, with brown wings and a white rump

Juvenile: same as female

Nest: cup; female builds; 1 brood per year

Eggs: 4-6; pale blue, unmarked

Incubation: 10-12 days; female incubates

Fledging: 11-17 days; female and male feed young

Migration: partial migrator, moves around North America in flocks of up to 20

Food: seeds, insects, will come to seed feeders

Compare: Confused with other winter birds. The Pine Siskin (pg. 75) has streaked chest and belly, and yellow wing bars. Female Purple Finch (pg. 85) has heavily streaked chest and white line above eye. Female House Finch (pg. 71) has a heavily streaked white chest.

Stan's Notes: Often called Wild Canary. Feeder bird that enjoys Nyjer thistle. Late summer nesting, uses silky down from wild thistle for nest. Appears roller-coaster-like in flight. Listen for them to twitter during flight. Almost always in small flocks. Moves only far enough south to find food. Small percentage stays all winter.

COMMON YELLOWTHROAT
Geothlypis trichas

SUMMER

Size: 5" (13 cm)

Male: An olive brown bird with a bright yellow throat and breast, and a white belly. Distinctive black mask outlined in white. Long, thin, pointed black bill.

Female: same as male, only lacking black mask

Juvenile: same as female

Nest: cup; female builds; 2 broods per year

Eggs: 3-5; white with brown markings

Incubation: 11-12 days; female incubates

Fledging: 10-11 days; female and male feed young

Migration: complete, to southern states and Central America

Food: insects

Compare: Found in a similar habitat as the American Goldfinch (pg. 249), but lacks the male's black forehead and wings. The male Yellow Warbler (pg. 255) has fine orange streaks on chest and lacks black mask. Yellow-rumped Warbler (pg. 173) only has spots of yellow, compared with Yellowthroat's yellow breast.

Stan's Notes: A common warbler of open fields and marshes. A frequent cowbird host. Young remain dependent upon parents longer than most warblers. It has a cheerful, well-known song, "witchity-witchity-witchity-witchity." Males perform a curious courtship display, bouncing in and out of tall grass while uttering an unusual song.

male

female

MAGNOLIA WARBLER
Dendroica magnolia

Size: 5" (13 cm)

Male: A yellow and black warbler with a white eyebrow and gray crown. White wing patch and yellow rump with obvious white patches on tail. Heavy black streaks on chest.

Female: similar to male, lacks black on face, has two white wing bars

Juvenile: same as female

Nest: cup; female and male build; 1 brood per year

Eggs: 3-5; white with brown markings

Incubation: 11-13 days; female incubates

Fledging: 8-10 days; female and male feed young

Migration: complete, to Central America

Food: insects

Compare: More yellow than Yellow-rumped Warbler (pg. 173). Look for the yellow chest and belly with heavy black streaks. The Yellow Warbler (pg. 255) lacks black back and face. Prairie Warbler (pg. 257) has olive back with chestnut-colored streaks.

Stan's Notes: One of the most common warblers in Indiana during spring (mid-May) and fall (late August) migrations. Look for them low in trees, where they feed on insects. Often fan their tails while picking insects from the underside of leaves. Males often feed higher up in trees than females. Nests throughout Canada and the northern states. Named by chance when ornithologist Alexander Wilson spotted the bird in a magnolia tree.

male

female

YELLOW WARBLER
Dendroica petechia

Size: 5" (13 cm)

Male: Yellow warbler with orange streaks on the chest and belly. Long, pointed dark bill.

Female: same as male, lacking orange streaking

Juvenile: similar to adult, only much duller

Nest: cup; female builds; 1 brood per year

Eggs: 4-5; white with brown markings

Incubation: 11-12 days; female incubates

Fledging: 10-12 days; female and male feed young

Migration: complete, to southern states, Mexico, Central and South Americas

Food: insects

Compare: Look for orange streaking on chest of male. The male American Goldfinch (pg. 249) has black wings and forehead. The female Yellow Warbler is similar to the female American Goldfinch (pg. 249), but lacks its white wing bars.

Stan's Notes: A common warbler of gardens and shrubby areas not far from water. Males are often seen higher up in trees than females. Females are less conspicuous. Starts to migrate south in July and is complete in August. Migrates at night in mixed flocks of other warblers. Rests and feeds during the day.

PRAIRIE WARBLER
Dendroica discolor

Size: 5" (13 cm)

Male: Olive back with chestnut-colored streaks. Bright yellow from the chin to belly. Black streaks on sides from the neck down. Black line through eye. Yellow eyebrow.

Female: same as male, only duller

Juvenile: similar to female

Nest: cup; female builds; 2 broods per year

Eggs: 3-5; white with brown markings

Incubation: 11-14 days; female incubates

Fledging: 8-11 days; female and male feed young

Migration: complete, to Caribbean

Food: insects

Compare: More black than Yellow Warbler (pg. 255) and less black than the Magnolia Warbler (pg. 253). Lacks the complete black mask of the Common Yellowthroat (pg. 251). Watch for the Prairie Warbler to twitch its tail when feeding.

Stan's Notes: A very common and widespread warbler in Indiana. Nests in dry, brushy clearings and forest edges, thus making it a perfect host for the Brown-headed Cowbird. Will sometimes desert a parasitized nest. Prairie Warblers return to Indiana in late April to mid-May in mixed flocks of warblers. Nests in upright fork of trees. Feeds young mainly caterpillars. Unfortunately, it was mis-named when it was first found in a barren area in Kentucky.

female

male pg. 231

SCARLET TANAGER
Piranga olivacea

SUMMER

Size:	7" (18 cm)
Female:	Drab greenish yellow with olive wings and tail. Whitish wing linings. Dark eye.
Male:	bright scarlet red bird with jet black wings and tail, ivory bill and dark eye
Juvenile:	same as female
Nest:	cup; female builds; 1 brood per year
Eggs:	4-5; blue green with brown markings
Incubation:	13-14 days; female incubates
Fledging:	9-11 days; female and male feed young
Migration:	complete, to Central and South Americas
Food:	insects, fruit
Compare:	Female Northern Cardinal (pg. 109) has black mask and red bill, but lacks the dark wings of the female Scarlet Tanager. Larger than female American Goldfinch (pg. 249) and lacks the Goldfinch's white wing bars. Female Baltimore Oriole (pg. 261) has gray brown wings and white wing bars.

Stan's Notes: Male sheds (molts) its bright red plumage in the fall, appearing more like the female. Prefers mature unbroken woodland, where it hunts for insects high in the tops of trees. Requires a minimum of four acres for nesting; prefers eight acres. Tropical-looking birds, they arrive late in spring and leave early in autumn. Scarlet Tanager is included in some 240 tanager species in the world. Nearly all are brightly colored and live in the tropics. The name "Tanager" comes from a South American Tupi Indian word meaning "any small, brightly colored bird."

259

male pg. 223

female

BALTIMORE ORIOLE
Icterus galbula

Size: 7-8" (18-20 cm)

Female: Pale yellow bird with gray brown wings, white wing bars. Gray bill and dark eye.

Male: bright, flaming orange bird with black head and black extending down nape of neck onto back, black wings with white and orange wing bars, orange tail with black streaks, gray bill and dark eye

Juvenile: same as female

Nest: pendulous; female builds; 1 brood per year

Eggs: 4-5; bluish with brown markings

Incubation: 12-14 days; female incubates

Fledging: 12-14 days; female and male feed young

Migration: complete, to Mexico, Central and South Americas

Food: insects, fruit, nectar, will come to orange halves and nectar feeders

Compare: The female Oriole is often confused with female Scarlet Tanager (pg. 259), which has olive-colored wings.

Stan's Notes: Fantastic songsters, these birds are often heard before seen. Easily attracted to a feeder offering grape jelly, orange halves or sugar water (nectar). Parents bring young to feeders. They build their sock-like nest at the outermost branches of tall trees. They often return to the same area year after year. Some of the last birds to arrive in spring (May) and first to leave in fall (September). They sit in the tops of the trees feeding on caterpillars.

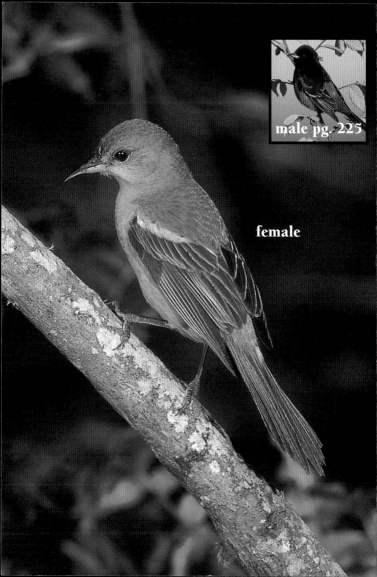

male pg. 225

female

ORCHARD ORIOLE
Icterus spurius

SUMMER

Size: 7-8" (18-20 cm)

Female: A olive green bird with a dull yellow belly, two white wing bars on dark gray wings. Long, thin black bill with a small gray mark on lower mandible (jaw).

Male: dull orange with a black head, chin, upper back, wings and tail, single white wing bar

Juvenile: same as female

Nest: pendulous; female builds; 1 brood per year

Eggs: 3-5; pale blue to white with brown markings

Incubation: 11-12 days; female and male incubate

Fledging: 11-14 days; female and male feed young

Migration: complete to Central Mexico and northern South America

Food: insects, fruit, comes to fruit/nectar feeders

Compare: Similar to female Baltimore Oriole (pg. 261), which has a brighter yellow belly, and female Scarlet Tanager (pg. 259), which has olive-colored wings.

Stan's Notes: Prefers open woods and orchards, hence its common name. They eat insects until wild fruits start to ripen. One of the last birds to arrive in spring and one of the first to leave each fall, spending only about three to four months in Indiana. More common in southern Indiana. Usually nests alone, but sometimes in small colonies. Parents bring young to jelly and orange half feeders shortly after fledging. Many people mistakenly think the orioles have left during summer, but in fact, the birds are concentrating on finding insects to feed their young.

male

female

EVENING GROSBEAK
Coccothraustes vespertinus

WINTER

Size: 8" (20 cm)

Male: A striking bird with a stocky body, large ivory-to-greenish bill, bright yellow eyebrows, a dirty yellow head, black-and-white wings and tail, and yellow rump and belly.

Female: similar to male, with softer colors, and gray head and throat

Juvenile: same as female, brown bill

Nest: cup; female builds; 1 brood per year

Eggs: 3-4; blue with brown markings

Incubation: 12-14 days; female incubates

Fledging: 13-14 days; female and male feed young

Migration: irruptive, moves around the state in search of food

Food: seeds, insects, fruit, comes to seed feeders

Compare: Larger than its close relative, the American Goldfinch (pg. 249). Look for the dark head with bright yellow eyebrow and extra large bill.

Stan's Notes: One of the largest finches. Has characteristic undulating finch-like flight. Has unusually large bill for cracking seeds, its main source of food. Often seen on gravel roads eating gravel, from which it gets minerals, salts and grit to grind up seeds it eats. Moves in large flocks in winter. Sheds outer layer of its bill in spring, exposing blue green bill. More numerous in some years than others.

EASTERN MEADOWLARK
Sturnella magna

Size: 9" (22.5 cm)

Male: A robin-shaped bird with brown back, lemon yellow chest and prominent black V-shaped necklace. White outer tail feathers.

Female: same as male

Juvenile: same as adult

Nest: cup, on the ground in dense cover; female builds; 2 broods per year

Eggs: 3-5; white with brown markings

Incubation: 13-15 days; female incubates

Fledging: 11-12 days; female and male feed young

Migration: complete, to Central America

Food: insects, seeds

Compare: The only large yellow bird with a black V mark on chest.

Stan's Notes: A bird of open grassy country. Best known for its wonderful song. Often seen perched on a fence post, it will quickly dive into tall grass when approached. Has conspicuous white markings on each side of its tail, most often seen when flying away. Nest is sometimes domed with dried grass. Called Meadowlark because it's a bird of meadows and sings like the larks of Europe. Eastern Meadowlark's song is a flute-like, clear whistle. Not a member of the lark family, it actually belongs to the blackbird family. Related to blackbirds, grackles and orioles.

HELPFUL RESOURCES:

Birder's Handbook, The. Ehrlich, Paul, David S. Dobkin and Darryl Wheye. New York: Simon and Schuster, 1988.

Birds Do It, Too: The Amazing Sex Life of Birds. Harrison, George and Kit Harrison. Minocqua, WI: Willow Creek Press, 1997.

Birds of Forest, Yard, and Thicket. Eastman, John. Mechanicsburg, PA: Stackpole Books, 1997.

Birds of Indiana, The. Mumford, Russell E. and Charles E. Keller. n.p.: Indiana University Press, 1984.

Birds of North America. Kaufman, Kenn. New York: Houghton Mifflin, 2000.

Cardinal, The. Osborne, June. Austin: University of Texas Press, 1995.

Cry of the Sandhill Crane, The. Grooms, Steve. Minocqua, WI: NorthWord Press, 1992.

Dictionary of American Bird Names, The. Choate, Ernest A. Boston: Harvard Common Press, 1985.

Everything You Never Learned About Birds. Rupp, Rebecca. Pownal, VT: Storey Publishing, 1997.

Field Guide to the Birds, A: A Completely New Guide to All the Birds of Eastern and Central North America. Peterson, Roger Tory and Virginia Marie Peterson. Boston: Houghton Mifflin, 1998.

Field Guide to the Birds of North America, Third Edition. Washington, DC: National Geographic Society, 1999.

Field Guide to Warblers of North America, A. Dunn, Jon and Kimball Garrett. Boston: Houghton Mifflin, 1997.

Folklore of Birds. Martin, Laura C. Old Saybrook, CT: Globe Pequot Press, 1996.

Guide to Bird Behavior, A: Vol I, II, III. Stokes, Donald and Lillian Stokes. Boston: Little, Brown and Company, 1989.

How Birds Migrate. Kerlinger, Paul. Mechanicsburg, PA: Stackpole Books, 1995.

Lives of Birds, The: Birds of the World and Their Behavior. Short, Lester L. Collingdale, PA: DIANE Publishing, 2000.

National Audubon Society: North American Birdfeeder Handbook. Burton, Robert. New York: Dorling Kindersley Publishing, 1995.

Photographic Guide to North American Raptors, A. Wheeler, Brian K. and William S. Clark. New York: Academic Press, 1999.

Secret Lives of Birds, The. Gingras, Pierre. Toronto: Key Porter Books, 1997.

Secrets of the Nest. Dunning, Joan. Boston: Houghton Mifflin, 1994.

Stokes Bluebird Book: The Complete Guide to Attracting Bluebirds. Stokes, Donald and Lillian Stokes. Boston: Little, Brown and Company, 1991.

Stokes Field Guide to Birds: Eastern Region. Stokes, Donald and Lillian Stokes. Boston: Little, Brown and Company, 1996.

Stokes Purple Martin Book. Stokes, Donald and Lillian Stokes. Boston: Little, Brown and Company, 1997.

INDIANA BIRDING HOTLINES:

To report unusual bird sightings or possibly hear recordings of where birds have been seen, you can often call pre-recorded hotlines detailing such information. Since these hotlines are usually staffed by volunteers, and phone numbers and even the organizations that host them often change, the phone numbers are not listed here. To obtain the numbers, go to your favorite internet search engine, type in something like "rare bird alert hotline Indiana" and follow the links provided.

WEB PAGES:

The internet is a valuable place to learn more about birds. You may find birding on the net a fun way to discover additional information or to spend a long winter night. These web sites will assist you in your pursuit of birds. If a web address doesn't work (they often change a bit), just enter the name of the group into a search engine to track down the new web address.

SITE	ADDRESS
Indiana Audubon Society	www.indianaaudubon.org
Sycamore Audubon Society	www.audubon.org/chapter/in/sycamore
Soarin' Hawk Raptor Rehabilitation	www.soarinhawk.org
American Birding Association	www.americanbirding.org
Cornell Lab of Ornithology	www.birds.cornell.edu
Author Stan Tekiela's home page	www.naturesmart.com

CHECK LIST/INDEX

Use the boxes to check the birds you've seen.

ABOUT THE AUTHOR:

Naturalist, wildlife photographer and writer Stan Tekiela is the originator of the popular state-specific field guides such as *Trees of Indiana Field Guide*. For over two decades, Stan has authored more than 100 field guides, nature appreciation books and wildlife audio CDs for nearly every state in the nation, presenting many species of birds, mammals, reptiles and amphibians, trees, wildflowers and cacti. Holding a Bachelor of Science degree in Natural History from the University of Minnesota and as an active professional naturalist for more than 20 years, Stan studies and photographs wildlife throughout the United States and has received various national and regional awards for his books and photographs. Also a well-known columnist and radio personality, his syndicated column appears in over 20 newspapers and his wildlife programs are broadcast on a number of Midwest radio stations. He is a member of the North American Nature Photography Association and Canon Professional Services. Stan resides in Victoria, Minnesota, with his wife, Katherine, and daughter, Abigail. He can be contacted via his web page at www.naturesmart.com.